Back to Basics™

YEARS 4 & 5

ADDITION AND SUBTRACTION

Do you need to know the basics of addition and subtraction? Let's learn about them together.

Parents and carers are encouraged to read the explanation and practice sections with their child.

Ann Baker

Illustrated by
Janice Bowles

About this book

Each unit in this book begins with a brief **explanation** of a concept or a strategy. You are encouraged to read this explanation with your child and, where appropriate, to use everyday materials and examples to give meaning to the concepts.

We practise is a worked example for you and your child to discuss together, paying particular attention to the thinking processes required to understand the concept or apply the strategy.

You practise gives your child the opportunity to practise the concept or strategy. It also indicates how well your child understands the new material and often includes problem-solving questions to ensure that your child has mastered the concept or strategy.

If further support is required, you and your child's teacher can devise a plan to ensure that all the basic concepts are fully understood and consolidated.

The **Tests** at the end of the book are provided to check that the concepts are fully understood. Test 1 can be done after units 1–10 are completed and Test 2 when the book is finished.

Meet 'BOB' – Back Of the Book

At the end of each unit, BOB reminds your child to go to the Answers section at the back of the book.

Mathematical Content

This book has been designed to cover the concepts of addition and subtraction that your child will encounter in **Year 4** and **Year 5**. The units provide a comprehensive coverage of the following Key Topics from the **Australian Curriculum: Mathematics**.

Australian Curriculum : Mathematics

YEAR 4	YEAR 5
Use equivalent number sentences involving addition and subtraction to find unknown quantities (ACMNA083)	Use efficient mental and written strategies and apply appropriate digital technologies to solve problems (ACMNA291)

© Australian Curriculum, Assessment and Reporting Authority 2010.

Contents & Checklist

WRITING and TALKING ABOUT ADDITION & SUBTRACTION

Addition

3 + 4 = 7 is a number sentence.

The **plus** sign, **+**, means **add** the numbers in an equation.

There are other words that have the same meaning as add.

3 **and** 4 **more**

3 **plus** 4

So you need to watch out for words that tell you that addition is required.

The word **makes** is also a word that is used in addition.

2 plus 2 **makes** 4

When a question asks you to **Find the total ...**, this also means that you need to **add** to find the answer.

Subtraction

6 – 3 = 3 is also a number sentence.

The minus sign, **–**, means **subtract** the second number from the first in an equation.

There are other words that have the same meaning as subtract.

6 **minus** 3

6 **take away** 3

Other words that tell you a question is a subtraction are **leaves** and **left**.

7 take away 2 **leaves** 5

If you take away 2 from 7, how many are **left**?

Equals

In an equation, the numbers on one side of an equals sign, **=**, must have the same value as, or **balance**, the numbers on the other side.

8 **balances** 3 + 5, so you can write this fact as an equation 8 = 3 + 5

3 + 5 **balances** 2 + 6, so you can write this fact as an equation 3 + 5 = 6 + 2

Watch out! The equals sign is usually followed by an answer, but not always. So think carefully about what the equals sign means and remember that it does not mean add or subtract.

GAME CARD IDEAS

Cut out the game cards – they will last longer if they are laminated. Here are some games for you to try.

Race to 300

Sort the cards into two piles – one for 10s and one for 1s. Put two Joker cards in each pile. When playing, the Jokers can be used to represent any number that the player chooses.

On their turn, players take a card from each pile and make a two-digit number, which they add on to their total to make a running score.

The winner is either the first player to make or pass 300 or the player who is closest to 300 when all cards have been used.

Highest Total Wins

Start by using only 1s, 10s or 100s according to the confidence level of the players. Shuffle the cards and deal each player two, three or four cards. Each player then adds the numbers to find their total. The player with the highest total wins a point.

Once players are confident, you can play with a mix of 1s, 10s and 100s.

Race to 3000

Extend Race to 3000 by including a pile of 100s cards, but put only one Joker in each pile.

Race Back from 300

Set up the cards as for Race to 300, but for this game each player starts with a total of 300 and uses subtraction to bring the total down towards zero.

The first player to reach zero or beyond is the winner.

A count-back strategy on an empty number line can help players with this game.

NOTE: Games are meant to be fun and provide practice without stress. It is recommended that you stop playing while you are still having fun and then your child will want to play again another time.

UNIT 1

EXTENDING BASIC NUMBER FACTS

The **basic facts** that you know for numbers up to 10 can be also used for larger numbers.

Rainbow facts to 10

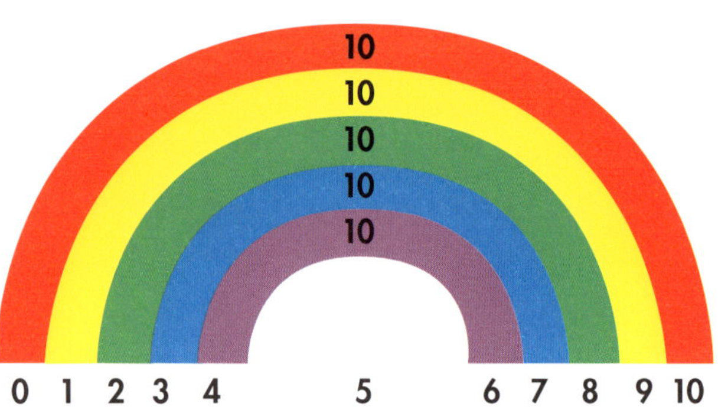

These are the rainbow pairs that add to 10.

Rainbow facts to 100

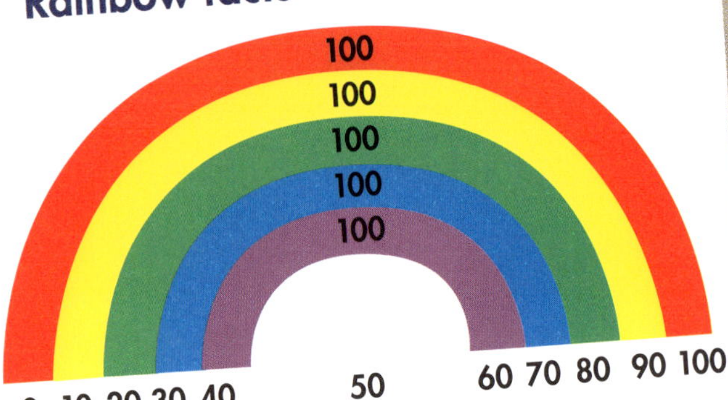

These are the rainbow pairs that add to 100. Do you notice the similarities?

For example:

6 + 4 = 10   60 + 40 = 100

You can also use doubles facts to help you with larger numbers. For example:

4 + 4 = 8   (double 4 equals 8)

40 + 40 = 80   (double 40 equals 80)

Near doubles are also useful. For example:

4 + 5 = 4 + 4 + 1 = 9   (4 + 5 is a near double)

40 + 50 = 40 + 40 + 10 = 90 (40 + 50 is a near double too)

We practise

Show how to use near doubles to work out 30 + 40.

30 + 30 + 10 = 70

40 + 40 − 10 = 70

Write the answer and the strategy you could use for each addition (rf for rainbow fact, d for double or nd for near double).

30 + 70 = 100 (rf)

60 + 50 = 110 (nd)

30 + 30 = 60 (d)

You practise

Show how to use near doubles for each of these additions.

1 20 + 30 ____ + ____ + ____ = ____
____ + ____ − ____ = ____

 50 + 40 ____ + ____ + ____ = ____
____ + ____ − ____ = ____

 60 + 70 ____ + ____ + ____ = ____
____ + ____ − ____ = ____

 80 + 90 ____ + ____ + ____ = ____
____ + ____ − ____ = ____

You practise

Write the answer and the strategy you could use for each addition (rf for rainbow fact, d for double or nd for near double).

 60 + 40 = ______ (____)

 70 + 70 = ______ (____)

 60 + 50 = ______ (____)

 80 + 20 = ______ (____)

 30 + 30 = ______ (____)

 70 + 80 = ______ (____)

It's always a good idea to use your basic facts when you are working with larger numbers.

BOB time!

UNIT 2

BRIDGING THROUGH 100

Knowing how to bridge through 10 helps with bridging through 100.

For example, to find **9 + 4**, you can **split** the 4 into 1 + 3. Then add 9 + 1 = 10, which is a **friendly number**, and then add 3 to find the answer, 10 + 3 = 13.

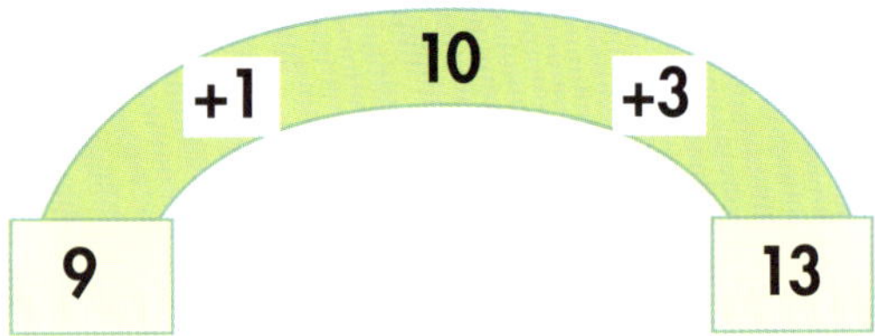

You can also use bridging for **90 + 40**. First split the 40 into 10 + 30. Add 90 + 10 = 100, which is a friendly number, and then add the 30 to find the answer, 100 + 30 = 130.

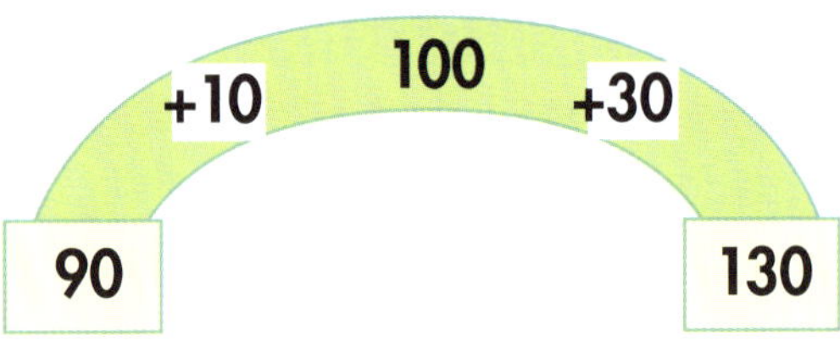

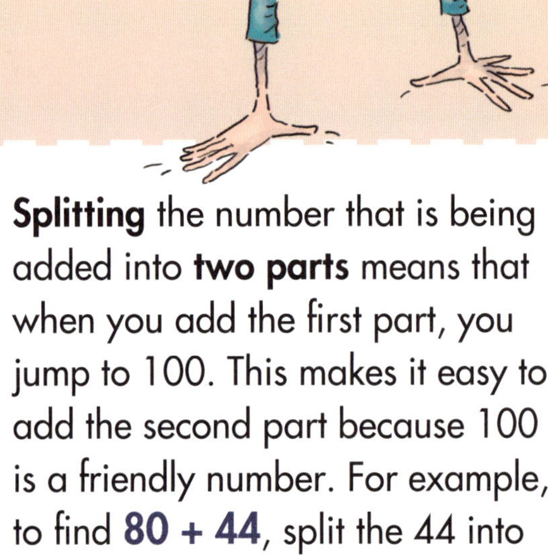

Splitting the number that is being added into **two parts** means that when you add the first part, you jump to 100. This makes it easy to add the second part because 100 is a friendly number. For example, to find **80 + 44**, split the 44 into 20 and 24 as shown below.

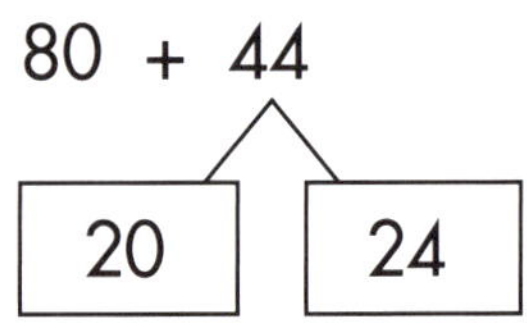

We practise

Show how the 6 in 9 + 6 should be split for a bridge through 10.

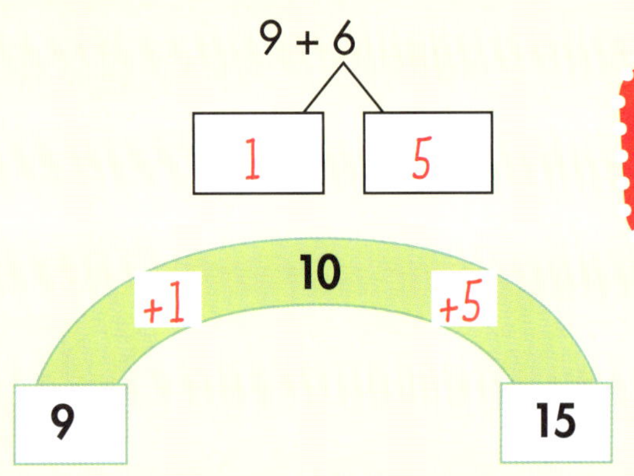

Show how the 60 in 80 + 60 should be split for a bridge through 100.

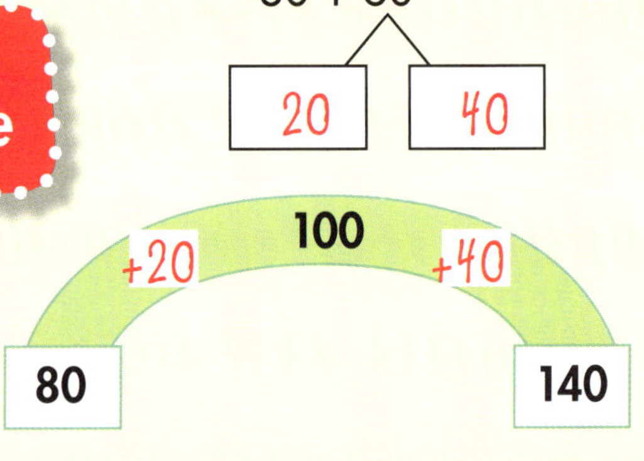

You practise

Show the number split and complete the bridge through 10 for each addition.

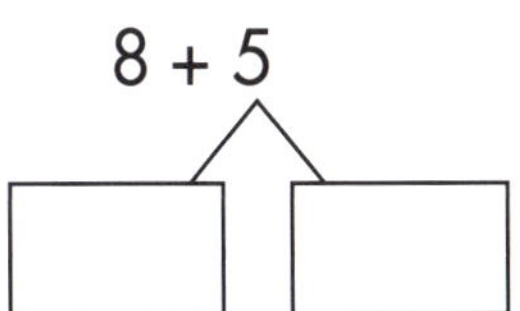
8 + 5

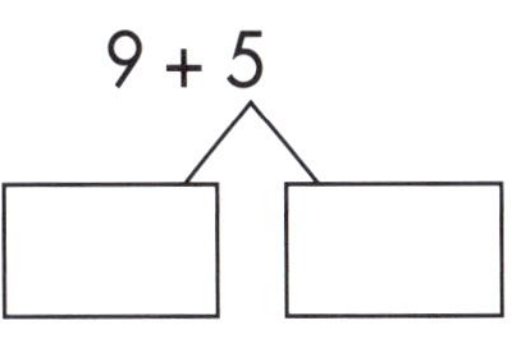
9 + 5

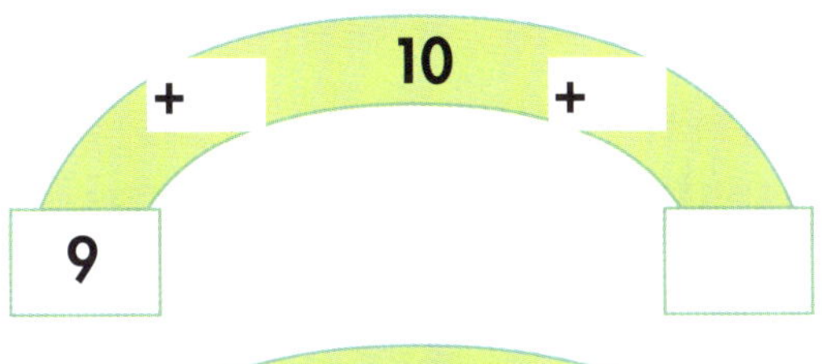

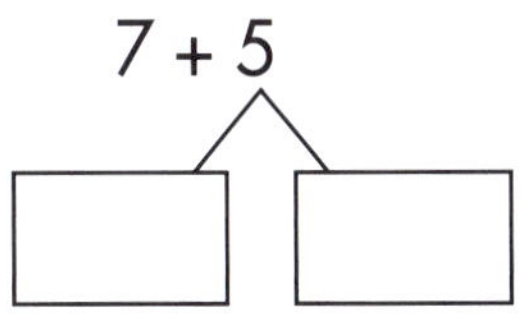
7 + 5

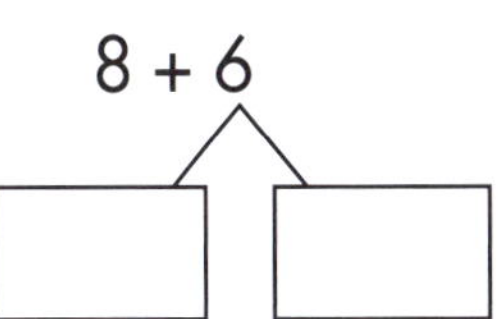
8 + 6

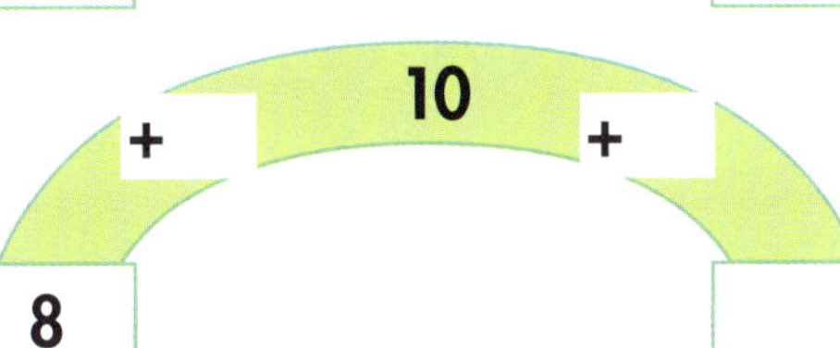

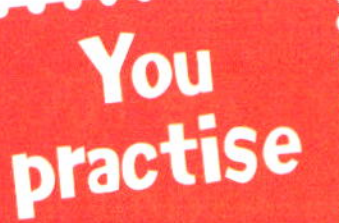

You practise

Show the number split and complete the bridge through 100 for each addition.

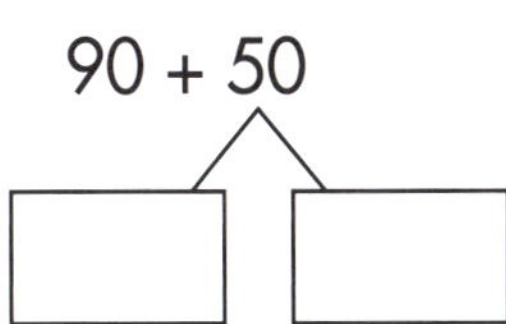
90 + 50

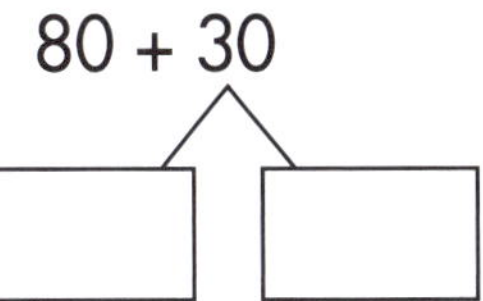
80 + 30

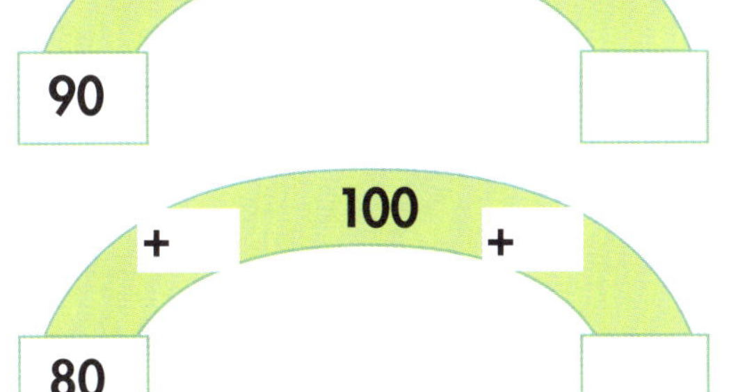

70 + 46

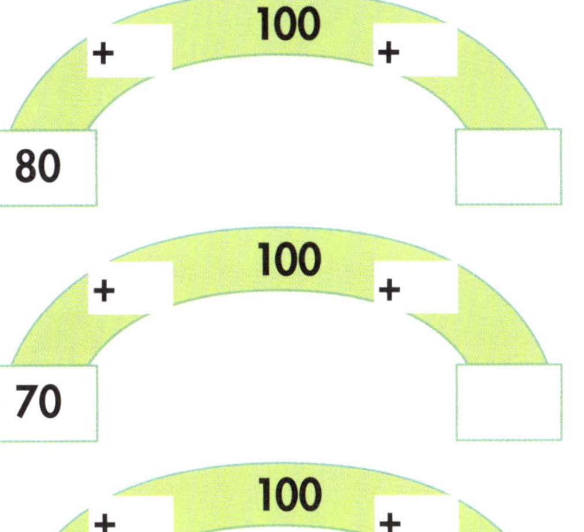

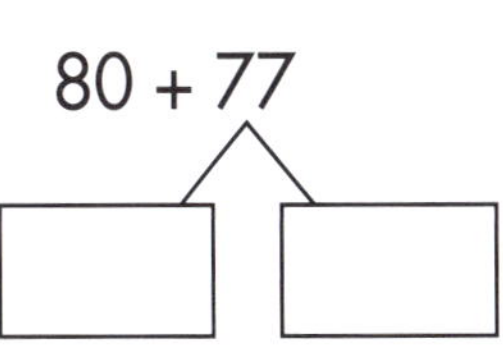
80 + 77

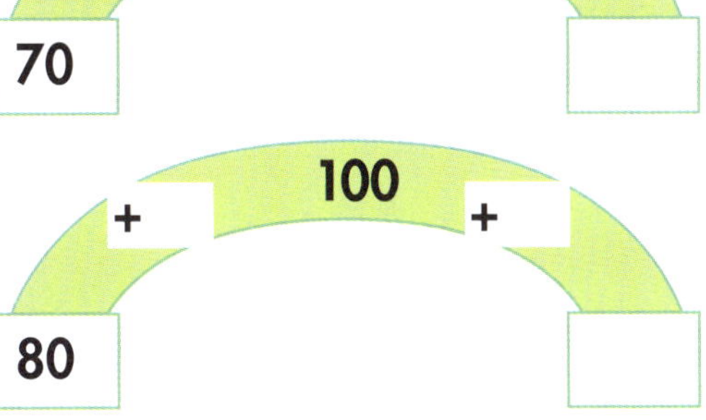

Remember to make the first step add to 100. After that the rest is easy.

BOB time!

ROUNDING AND ESTIMATING

When you are shopping, it is important to know if you have enough money to pay for what you want to buy. For example, if you have a $50 note and want to buy a game for $24 and a T-shirt for $35, you do not need to work out the full addition.

$24
+ $35

All you need is an **estimate** to see if you have enough money.

$20 + $30 = $50

This tells you that you do not have enough money to buy both items.

Always have an estimate in your mind before you do an addition.

To make an estimate for **29 + 31 + 42**, round each number up or down to the nearest 10. Use the rule that numbers ending in 1, 2, 3 or 4 round **down** to the 10 below and numbers ending in 5, 6, 7, 8 or 9 round **up** to the 10 above.

29 + 31 + 42
↓ ↓ ↓
30 + 30 + 40 = 100

An **estimate** for the addition is 100, so the actual answer will be **close to** 100.

We practise

Round these numbers to the nearest 10 to make an estimate for this addition.

43 + 56
↓ ↓
40 + 60 = 100

An estimate is 100

Round these numbers to the nearest 10 to make an estimate for this addition.

28 + 41 + 39
↓ ↓ ↓
30 + 40 + 40 = 110

An estimate is 110

You practise

Round these numbers to the nearest 10 to make an estimate for each addition.

1. 42 + 43
   ____ + ____ = ____ An estimate is ____

2. 34 + 52
   ____ + ____ = ____ An estimate is ____

3. 65 + 51
   ____ + ____ = ____ An estimate is ____

4. 73 + 62
   ____ + ____ = ____ An estimate is ____

5. 29 + 42 + 36
   ____ + ____ + ____ = ____ An estimate is ____

6. 37 + 28 + 29
   ____ + ____ + ____ = ____ An estimate is ____

7. 42 + 55 + 63
   ____ + ____ + ____ = ____ An estimate is ____

8. 32 + 21 + 18
   ____ + ____ + ____ = ____ An estimate is ____

9. 56 + 73 + 34
   ____ + ____ + ____ = ____ An estimate is ____

10. 98 + 52 + 48
    ____ + ____ + ____ = ____ An estimate is ____

Remember that a number ending in 5 rounds **up** to the 10 above.

Use your calculator to find out how close the estimates are to the actual answer.

BOB time!

ROUND and ADJUST for ADDITION

You can use rounding when making an estimate, but rounding can also be used to work out the exact answer to an addition.

Here is an example. **29 + 36**

Round 29 + 36 (29 +1 → 30)

30 + 36 = 66

Adjust 66 − 1 = 65

66 is too much because 1 was added to **round** 29 up to 30. So you need to **adjust** the addition by subtracting 1 from 66 to find the exact answer.

Rounding to a friendly number makes the addition much easier.

Here is another example that shows the steps for the **round and adjust** strategy.

37 + 45

Round 37 + 45 (37 +3 → 40)

40 + 45 = 85

Adjust 85 − 3 = 82

Show how to round and adjust to work out this addition.

38 + 53 (38 + 2 → 40)

Round 40 + 53 = 93

Adjust 93 − 2 = 91

We practise

Round and adjust in your head to work out this addition.

49 + 26 = 75

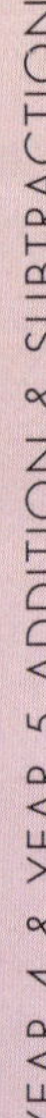

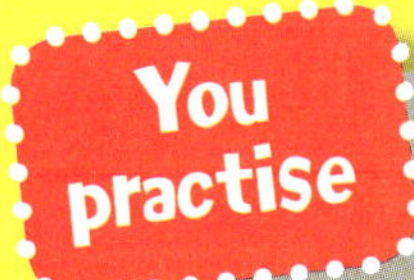

You practise

Show how to round and adjust to work out each addition.

1 39 + 27 (39 ↓ +___ , 27 ↓)

Round ___ + ___ = _____

Adjust ___ − ___ = _____

2 18 + 26 (18 ↓ +___ , 26 ↓)

Round ___ + ___ = _____

Adjust ___ − ___ = _____

3 27 + 35 (27 ↓ +___ , 35 ↓)

Round ___ + ___ = _____

Adjust ___ − ___ = _____

4 28 + 54 (28 ↓ +___ , 54 ↓)

Round ___ + ___ = _____

Adjust ___ − ___ = _____

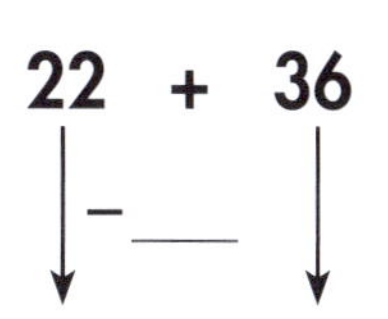

5 22 + 36 (22 ↓ −___ , 36 ↓)

Round ___ + ___ = _____

Adjust ___ + ___ = _____

6 31 + 47 (31 ↓ −___ , 47 ↓)

Round ___ + ___ = _____

Adjust ___ + ___ = _____

You practise

Round and adjust in your head to work out each addition.

7 48 + 23 = _____

8 37 + 26 = _____

9 23 + 48 = _____

10 42 + 37 = _____

Remember that if you **round down**, you need to **adjust** by **adding on**.

BOB time!

UNIT 5

LANDMARK NUMBERS

If there is a landmark number in an **addition**, it can make it easy to find the right answer.

25, 50, 75 and 100 are called landmark numbers because they are easy to work with and can help you with some additions.

As you can see by these combinations, landmark numbers are related in a special way.

25 + 25 = 50   25 + 50 = 75   25 + 75 = 100

50 + 50 = 100   50 + 75 = 125   75 + 75 = 150

For example, knowing that 25 + 75 = 100 can help you find the answer to **26 + 75**.

26 + 75

1 + 25 + 75 = 101

100

250, 500 and 750 are also landmark numbers. They can make complicated additions easier to work out.

For example:

260 + 270

10 + 250 + 250 + 20 = 530

500

We practise

Show how landmark numbers can be used to find the answer to these additions.

76 + 26

1 + 75 + 25 + 1 = 102

100

252 + 756

2 + 250 + 750 + 6 = 1008

1000

You practise

Show how landmark numbers can help with each addition.

26 + 77

___ + ___ + ___ + ___ = ___

___

51 + 27

___ + ___ + ___ + ___ = ___

___

78 + 76

___ + ___ + ___ + ___ = ___

___

51 + 76

___ + ___ + ___ + ___ = ___

___

253 + 251

___ + ___ + ___ + ___ = ___

___

503 + 506

___ + ___ + ___ + ___ = ___

___

751 + 253

___ + ___ + ___ + ___ = ___

___

752 + 503

___ + ___ + ___ + ___ = ___

___

Remember to look for the landmark numbers.

BOB time!

UNIT 6 TWO WAYS of ADDING QUICKLY

Number splitting and chunking can help you add numbers quickly, but you have to be comfortable about the idea of adding on to a friendly number.

For example, for **36 + 47**, first **split** 47 into 40 and 7 and then **add** the **chunks**.

36 + 47

36 + 40 = 76

76 + 7 = 83

The same method can be used for larger numbers. For example, for **156 + 35**, **split** the 35 into 30 and 5 and then **add** the **chunks**.

156 + 35

156 + 30 = 186

186 + 5 = 191

Adding the 10s first means that the answer will be close by.

Another method for showing these additions is the front end method.

Start by adding the leading digits and then add the rest.

	36		156
	+ 47		+ 35
The front end is 30 + 40 =	70	The front end is 150 + 30 =	180
	13		11
	83		191

We practise

Show how to work out 47 + 38 using number splitting and chunking.

47 + 38

47 + 30 = 77

77 + 8 = 85

Show how to work out 48 + 24 using the front-end method.

48

+ 24

40 + 20 = 60

12

72

You practise

Show the number split and chunking for these additions.

 56 + 33

 38 + 24

 27 + 68

 64 + 29

 37 + 46

 52 + 68

You practise

Show how to do these additions using the front-end method.

$$\begin{array}{r} 43 \\ +\ 76 \\ \hline \end{array}$$

$$\begin{array}{r} 38 \\ +\ 27 \\ \hline \end{array}$$

$$\begin{array}{r} 156 \\ +\ 58 \\ \hline \end{array}$$

$$\begin{array}{r} 235 \\ +\ 69 \\ \hline \end{array}$$

UNIT 7

ROUND AND ADJUST for SUBTRACTION

Round and adjust also works for subtraction.

For example, to find the answer to **46 – 29**, first round 29 up to 30, then subtract the 30, and adjust by adding 1 (because you subtracted 1 too many).

46 – 29

+1

Round **46 – 30 = 16**

Adjust **16 + 1 = 17**

You can check this answer by adding 17 + 29.

$$\begin{array}{r} 17 \\ +\ 29 \\ \hline 30 \\ 16 \\ \hline 46 \end{array}$$

Spot on!

Here is another example with a bit of a twist.

67 – 38

+1

Round **68 – 38 = 30**

Adjust **30 – 1 = 29**

68 – 38 is easy. But don't forget to adjust by subtracting 1, because 68 is 1 too many.

Show how to work out 57 – 19 using round and adjust.

57 – 19

+1

Round 57 – 20 = 37

Adjust 37 + 1 = 38

Show how to work out 47 – 28 using round and adjust.

47 – 28

+1

Round 48 – 28 = 20

Adjust 20 – 1 = 19

You practise

Show how to work out each subtraction using round and adjust.

1. 55 − 29

Round ___ − ___ = _____

Adjust ___ + ___ = _____

2. 76 − 28

Round ___ − ___ = _____

Adjust ___ + ___ = _____

3. 57 − 38

Round ___ − ___ = _____

Adjust ___ + ___ = _____

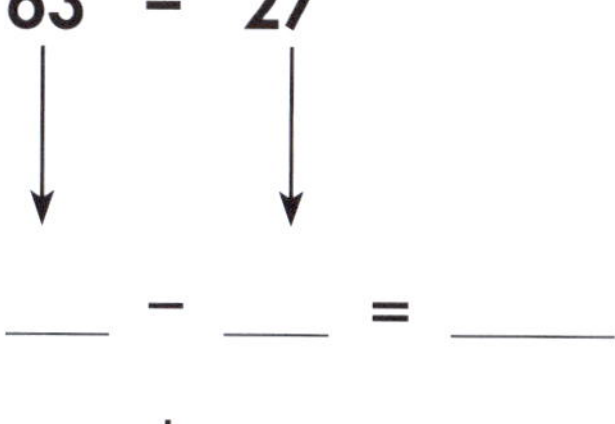

4. 63 − 27

Round ___ − ___ = _____

Adjust ___ + ___ = _____

5. 82 − 58

Round ___ − ___ = _____

Adjust ___ + ___ = _____

6. 77 − 29

Round ___ − ___ = _____

Adjust ___ + ___ = _____

7. 37 − 19

Round ___ − ___ = _____

Adjust ___ + ___ = _____

8. 46 − 27

Round ___ − ___ = _____

Adjust ___ + ___ = _____

9. 93 − 54

Round ___ − ___ = _____

Adjust ___ − ___ = _____

10. 87 − 55

Round ___ − ___ = _____

Adjust ___ − ___ = _____

BOB time!

ADDITION on a NUMBER LINE

An empty number line is a line with numbers marked to show mathematical operations like addition or subtraction.

It can be used to show an addition such as **36 + 25** in a way that makes the thinking clear.

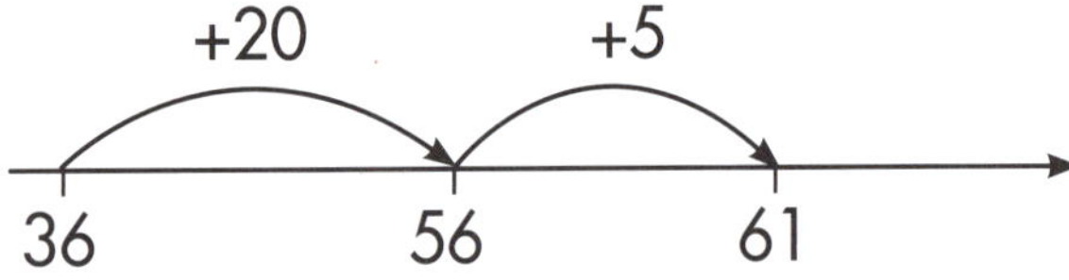

You could also use the empty number line to work out **36 + 49**.

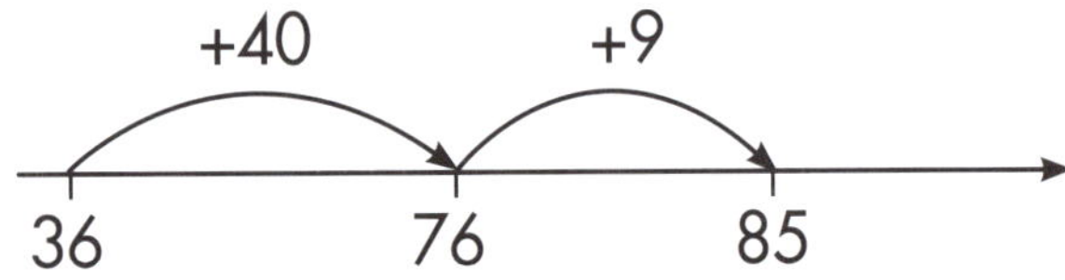

But if you decided to round the 49 up to 50 to help you work out the answer, you would have to adjust by subtracting 1. Here is how this looks on a number line.

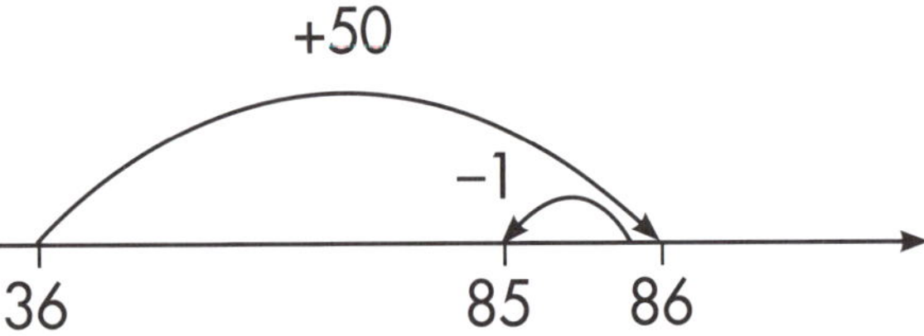

We practise

Show how to work out 47 + 46 using an empty number line.

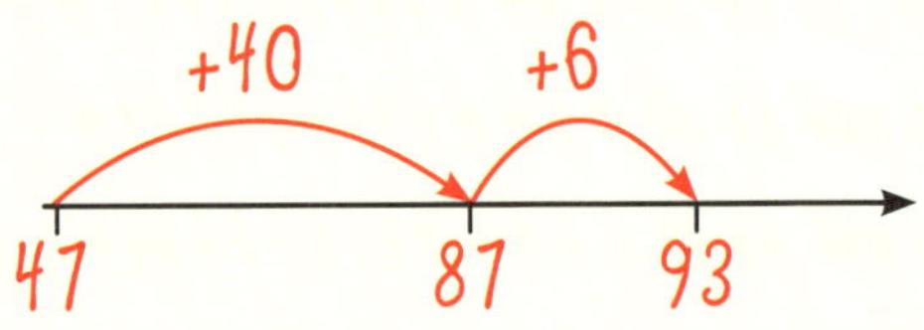

Show how to work out 27 + 68 using an empty number line and the round and adjust strategy.

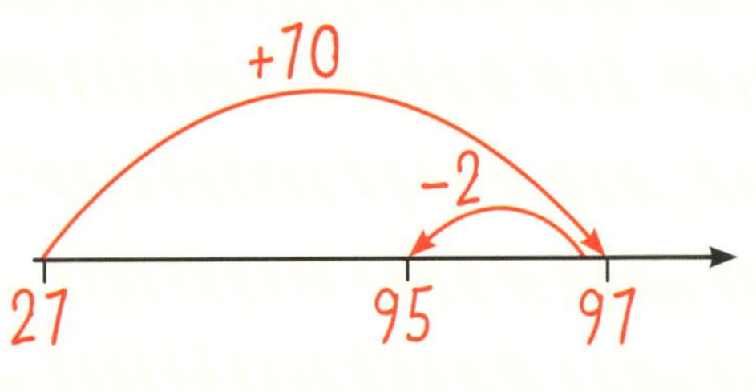

Did you notice the little **jump back** on the line? Adding 50 is 1 too many, so 1 was subtracted to get to the right answer.

You practise Show how to work out each addition using an empty number line.

47 + 36

54 + 35

38 + 27

64 + 67

73 + 65

Show how to work out each addition using an empty number line and the round and adjust strategy.

26 + 58

35 + 49

67 + 21

73 + 29

86 + 72

Remember to count back or count on after you round down.

BOB time!

UNIT 9

SUBTRACTION on a NUMBER LINE

An empty number line can also be used to work out subtractions.

For example, this number line shows how you can work out **46 – 27** by splitting 27 into 20 and 7.

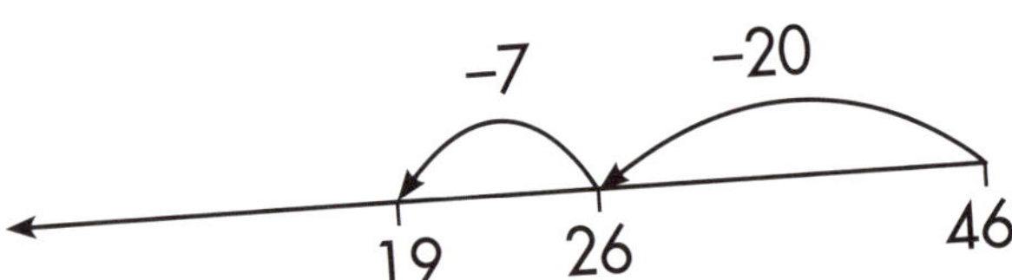

You could also use the round and adjust strategy.

First **round** 27 to 30, then subtract 30 from 46 to get 16, and **adjust** by adding 3.

You can show this thinking on an empty number line.

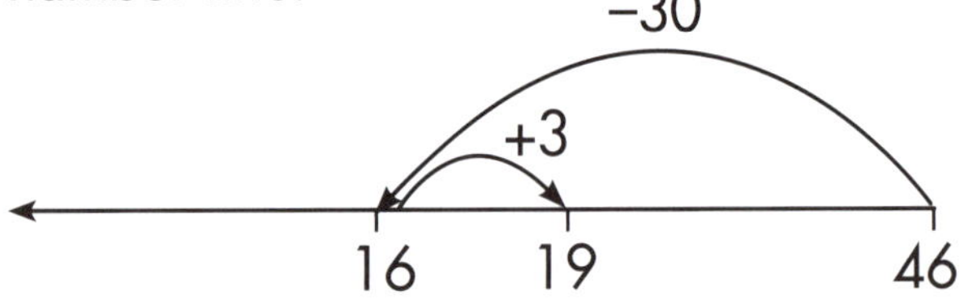

Whichever method you use, remember that friendly numbers are easy to subtract.

We practise

Work out 54 – 36 using an empty number line, without using the round and adjust strategy.

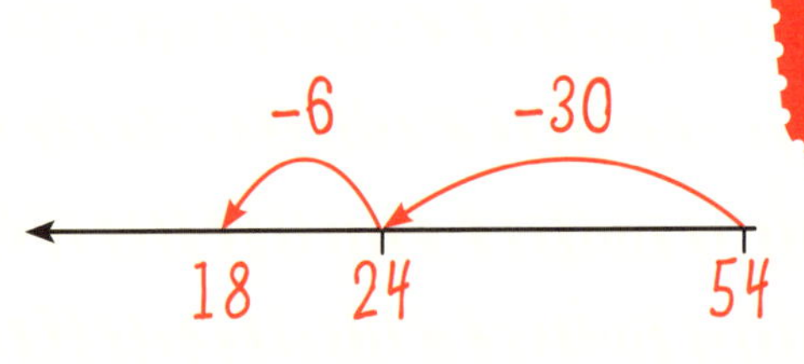

Work out 54 – 36 using an empty number line using the round and adjust strategy.

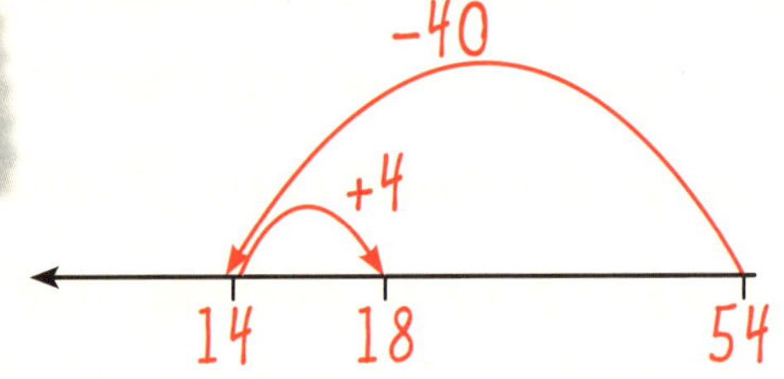

You practise

Work out each subtraction using an empty number line, **without** using the round and adjust strategy.

43 – 18

54 – 17

67 – 28

86 – 57

103 – 49

Remember to always check your answer with an addition.

You practise

Work out each subtraction using an empty number line using the round and adjust strategy.

43 – 18

54 – 17

67 – 28

86 – 57

103 – 49

BOB time!

PROBLEM SOLVING

Clare, Jake, Matty and Tsai are playing a game with Avatar cards.

Clare's Avatars have attack values of 32 and 49. Jake's Avatars have values of 25 and 54. Matty's Avatars have values of 53 and 31. The values of Tsai's Avatars are 58 and 43.

Who has the highest attack value? By how much is that player ahead of the player with the lowest attack value?

Notice that the important information is highlighted in blue and what has to be found out is highlighted in pink.

Here is the addition for each player's values and a good strategy to work out each total.

Player	Addition	Strategy	Working out	Total
Clare	32 + 49	Round and adjust	32 + 50 = 82	
			82 − 1 = 81	81
Jake	25 + 54	Landmark Numbers	25 + 50 = 75	
			75 + 4 = 79	79
Matty	53 + 31	Round and adjust	53 + 30 = 83	
			83 + 1 = 84	84
Tsai	58 + 43	Round and adjust	60 + 43 = 103	
			103 − 2 = 101	101

Tsai has the highest attack value (101) and Jake has the lowest (79). To find out how much Tsai is ahead of Jake, you need to work out **101 − 79**.

Look at this subtraction on an empty number line.

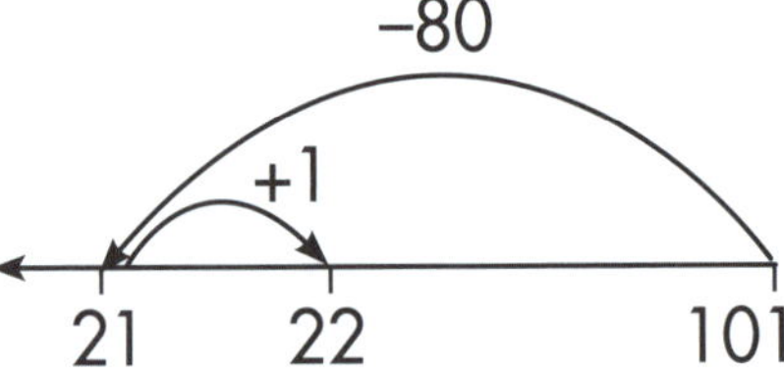

Tsai is 22 attack values ahead of Jake.

We practise

For this problem, highlight the important information in blue and what you have to find out in pink. Use an empty number line to show how you found the answer.

Clare's Avatars have 61 more attack values than Jake's. Jake's Avatars have values of 24 and 17. What is the total of Clare's Avatars?

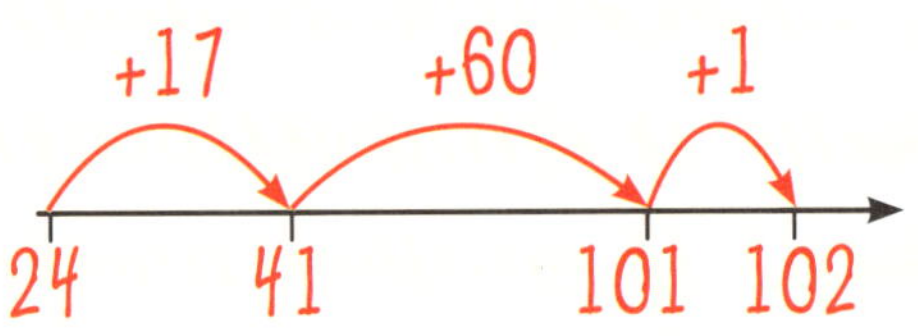

Clare's total is 102.

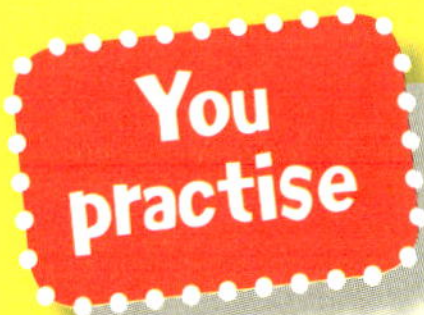

Highlight the important information and what you have to find out. Then answer each problem in a sentence.

UNIT 10

Jake has 57 collector cards. Clare has 19 less than Jake. How many collector cards do they have altogether?

Matty is playing darts with his Dad. Dad is leading by 47 points. Then Matty throws 6, 17 and double 13. Who is in the lead now and by how many points?

Clare has \$100. She wants to buy a game for \$25, a book for \$19 and a pair of sandals for \$60. Does she have enough money?

The bill is \$65. Clare pays \$20. How much is left for Jake and Matty to pay?

Closest to 100 is Clare and Jake's favourite game. They can throw four dice each and arrange them to make an addition. Clare has 62 + 15 and Jake has 43 + 54. Who is closest to 100 and by how much?

Clare's Avatar has a defence value of 48. Jake's has a value of 39. Jake and Clare are up against Matty's star card of 100 points. How much will they lose by?

Clare has \$65 now that Jake has paid back the \$18 he owed her. How much did Clare have before?

Matty and Ian are playing cards. Matty scores 117 with his first three cards. His first card is worth 29. His second card is worth 36. What is his third card worth?

Rebecca has made 144 muffins. 36 are for a coffee shop and 24 are for a morning tea. How many muffins are left?

Mrs Brown's Year 1 class are having a party on the 100th day of school. Today is Day 67. How many days until the party?

THREE-DIGIT ADDITIONS

The **front-end method** (see Unit 6) also works when you are working out **three-digit additions**.

Look at this example.

	345
	+ 236
Add the **100s** first	500
Add the **10s** next	70
Then add the **1s**	11
	581

200 + 300 = 500 and 40 + 30 = 70, so that's 570. I can do that in my head!

You can do this addition with one less step if you **combine** the **100s** and **10s**.

	345
	+ 236
Add the **100s** and **10s** first	570
Then add the **1s**	11
	581

We practise

Use the front-end method to work out this three-digit addition in **three** steps.

257
+ 348
500
90
15
605

Use the front-end method to work out this three-digit addition in **two** steps.

357
+ 458
800
15
815

Back to Basics

ADDITION & SUBTRACTION

YEARS 4 and 5

Back to Basics
ADDITION & SUBTRACTION
YEARS 4 and 5

Back to Basics
ADDITION & SUBTRACTION
YEARS 4 and 5

Back to Basics
ADDITION & SUBTRACTION
YEARS 4 and 5

Back to Basics
ADDITION & SUBTRACTION
YEARS 4 and 5

Back to Basics
ADDITION & SUBTRACTION
YEARS 4 and 5

Back to Basics
ADDITION & SUBTRACTION
YEARS 4 and 5

Back to Basics
ADDITION & SUBTRACTION
YEARS 4 and 5

Back to Basics
ADDITION & SUBTRACTION
YEARS 4 and 5

Back to Basics
ADDITION & SUBTRACTION
YEARS 4 and 5

Back to Basics
ADDITION & SUBTRACTION
YEARS 4 and 5

Back to Basics
ADDITION & SUBTRACTION
YEARS 4 and 5

Back to Basics
ADDITION & SUBTRACTION
YEARS 4 and 5

Back to Basics
ADDITION & SUBTRACTION
YEARS 4 and 5

Back to Basics
ADDITION & SUBTRACTION
YEARS 4 and 5

Back to Basics
ADDITION & SUBTRACTION
YEARS 4 and 5

1	2	3	4
5	6	7	8
9	0	10	20
30	40	50	60

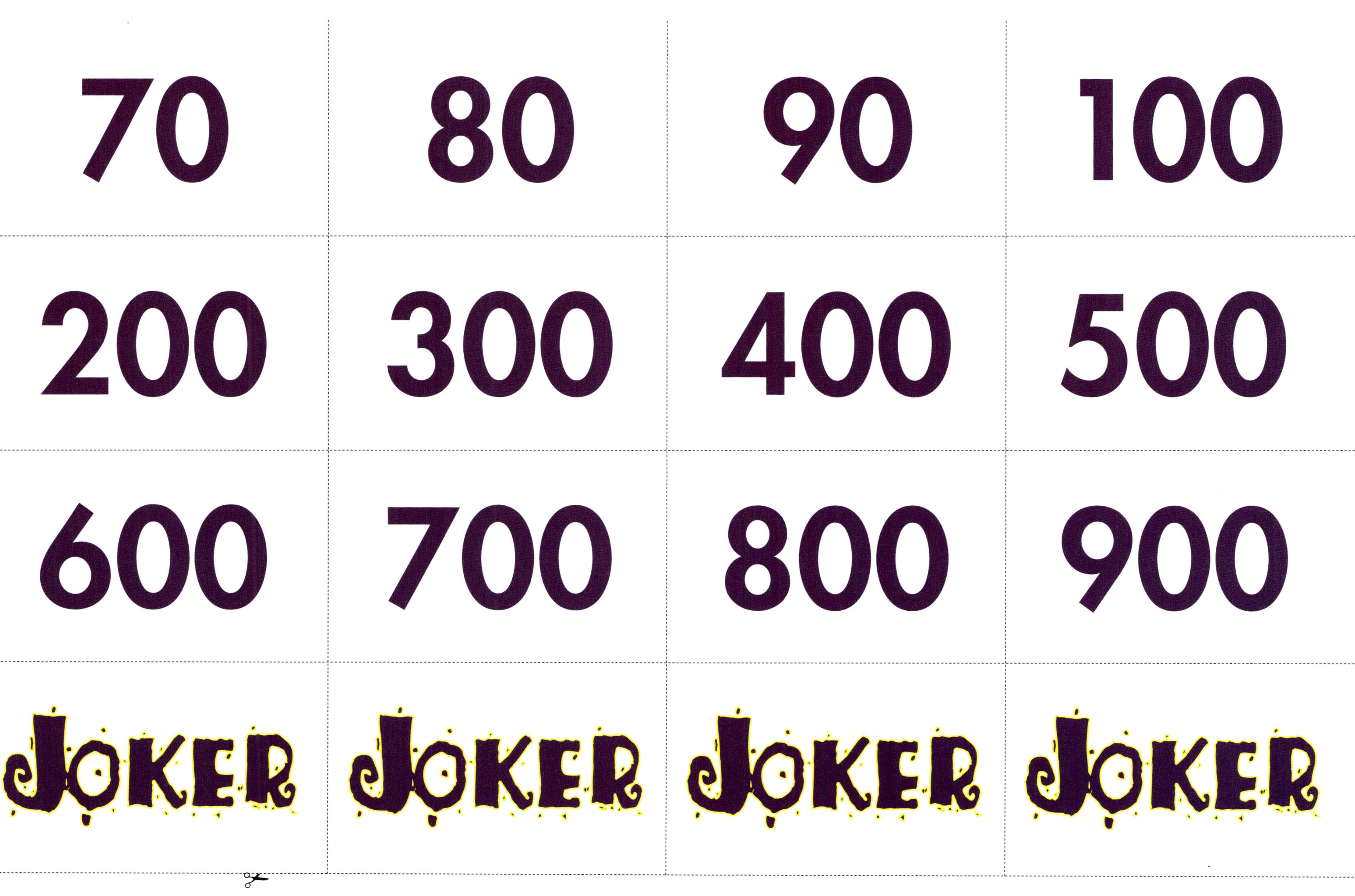
70
80
90
100
200
300
400
500
600
700
800
900
JOKER
JOKER
JOKER
JOKER

Back to Basics

ADDITION & SUBTRACTION

YEARS 4 and 5

Back to Basics
ADDITION & SUBTRACTION
YEARS 4 and 5
Back to Basics
ADDITION & SUBTRACTION
YEARS 4 and 5
Back to Basics
ADDITION & SUBTRACTION
YEARS 4 and 5
Back to Basics
ADDITION & SUBTRACTION
YEARS 4 and 5
Back to Basics
ADDITION & SUBTRACTION
YEARS 4 and 5
Back to Basics
ADDITION & SUBTRACTION
YEARS 4 and 5
Back to Basics
ADDITION & SUBTRACTION
YEARS 4 and 5
Back to Basics
ADDITION & SUBTRACTION
YEARS 4 and 5
Back to Basics
ADDITION & SUBTRACTION
YEARS 4 and 5
Back to Basics
ADDITION & SUBTRACTION
YEARS 4 and 5
Back to Basics
ADDITION & SUBTRACTION
YEARS 4 and 5
Back to Basics
ADDITION & SUBTRACTION
YEARS 4 and 5
Back to Basics
ADDITION & SUBTRACTION
YEARS 4 and 5
Back to Basics
ADDITION & SUBTRACTION
YEARS 4 and 5
Back to Basics
ADDITION & SUBTRACTION
YEARS 4 and 5

You practise

Work out each three-digit addition in three steps.

326
+ 142

272
+ 346

175
+ 434

189
+ 327

353
+ 228

367
+ 148

Watch out for rainbow facts and landmark numbers.

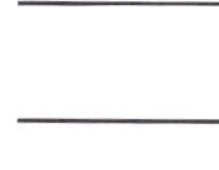

You practise

Work out each three-digit addition in two steps.

326
+ 142

257
+ 258

178
+ 136

763
+ 259

THREE-DIGIT SUBTRACTION

It helps if you cross off the numbers as you subtract them.

Let's see how number splitting can help with subtracting one three-digit number from another.

In this example, the 'thinking' steps are in **red** so you know what is happening at each step.

	254
	−136
254 − 100 leaves	154
154 − 30 leaves	124
124 − 6 (4 + 2) leaves	118

So the answer is 254 − 136 = 118.

Splitting 70 into 30 + 40 makes it much easier to subtract from 336. Can you see why?

Here's another example, but this time there is one more number split in the 'thinking' steps.

	436
	−178
436 − 100 leaves	336
336 − 70 (30 + 40) leaves	266
266 − 8 (6 + 2) leaves	258

So the answer is 436 − 178 = 258.

We practise

Use number splitting to work out this subtraction and show the 'thinking' steps.

	364
	−158
364 − 100 leaves	264
264 − 50 leaves	214
214 − 8 (4 + 4) leaves	206

364 − 158 = 206

Use number splitting to work out this subtraction, but leave out the 'thinking' steps.

327
− 148
227
187
179

327 − 148 = 179

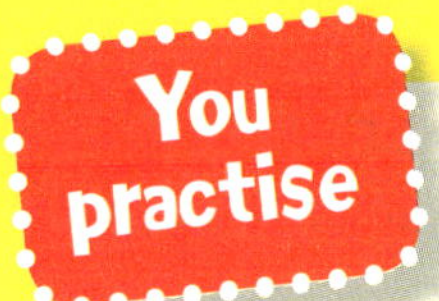

Use number splitting to work out each subtraction and show the 'thinking' steps.

465
− 323
leaves
leaves
leaves

656
− 238
leaves
leaves
leaves

Remember to split the 10s and the 1s if you need to.

534
− 126
leaves
leaves
leaves

735
− 419
leaves
leaves
leaves

367
− 148
leaves
leaves
leaves

673
− 427
leaves
leaves
leaves

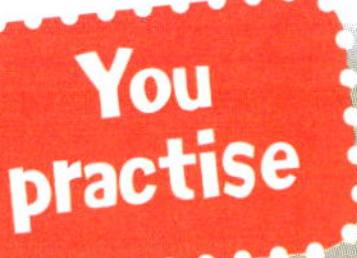

Use number splitting to work out each subtraction, but leave out the 'thinking' steps.

424
− 136

738
− 559

FIND THE DIFFERENCE

Finding the difference between two numbers really means finding the 'gap' between them.

Look at this simple example – it shows that the **difference** between 2 and 6 is 4.

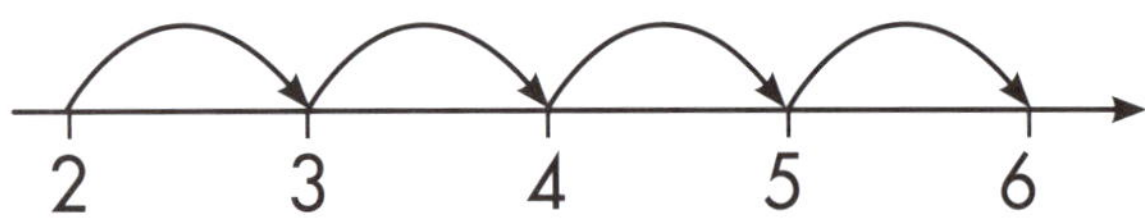

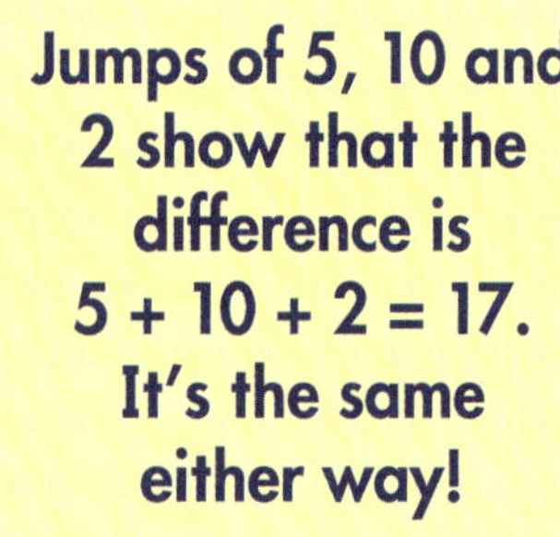

You can also add or subtract to find the difference between two numbers.

This example shows how to **count on** (add) from the smallest number to find the difference between 18 and 35.

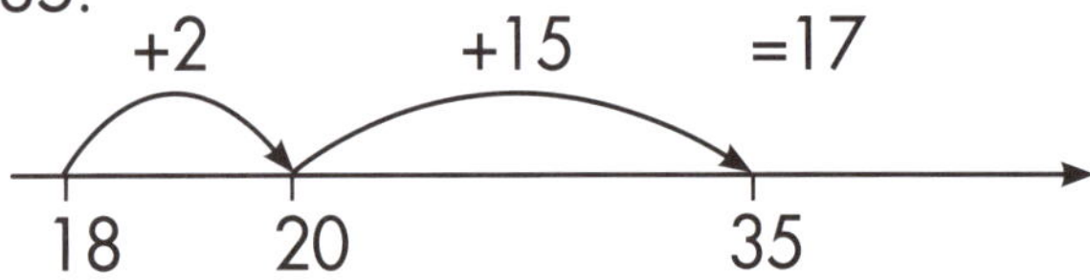

The difference between 18 and 35 is 17.

The difference can also be found by counting back (subtracting).

Look at this example.

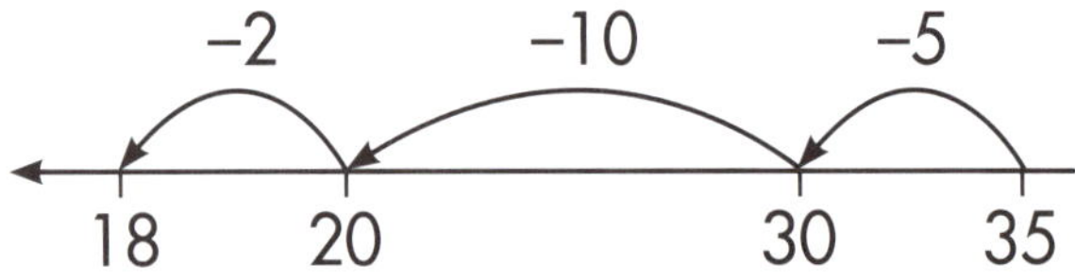

We practise

Find the difference between 24 and 59 using a count on strategy on an empty number line.

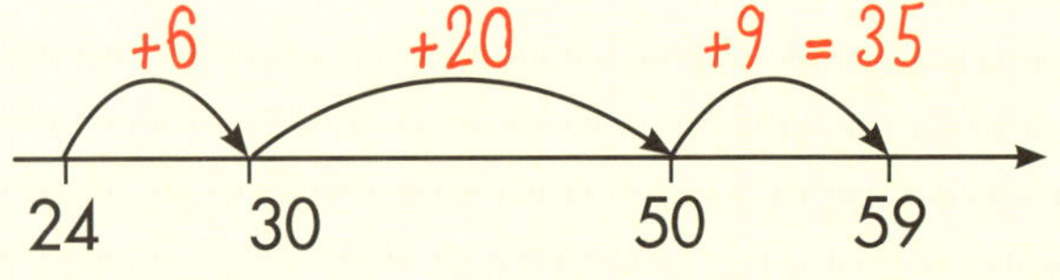

The difference is 35.

Find the difference between 24 and 59 using a count back strategy on an empty number line.

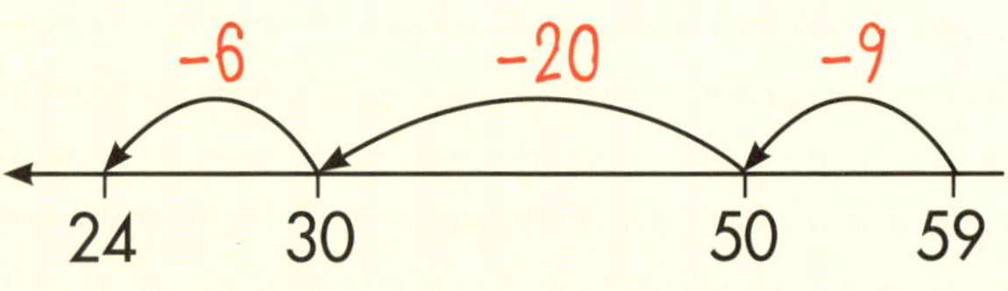

The difference is 35.

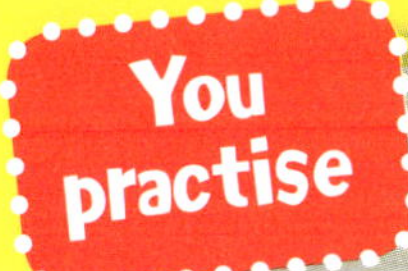

Find the difference between each pair of numbers using a count on strategy on an empty number line.

1. 27 and 42

   The difference is ______

2. 45 and 68

   The difference is ______

3. 37 and 116

   The difference is ______

You practise

Find the difference between each pair of numbers using a count back strategy on an empty number line.

See if you can find where two jumps are enough.

4. 27 and 42

   The difference is ______

5. 45 and 68

   The difference is ______

6. 37 and 116

   The difference is ______

BOB time!

UNIT 14

SIDEWAYS CHUNKING for ADDITION

When you have to add a list of numbers, it helps if you have smart strategies to find the total.

For example, spotting combinations that add to 10 or 100 can make finding the total much easier. You can also use **sideways chunking** to show where the 10s and 100s come from.

Look at this example to see how it works.

Spot the 10s first

47, 86, 34, 55, + 23 — 6 + 4 = 10, 7 + 3 = 10, = 25

Then spot the 100s

120 (47 + 86 … wait see below)

47 and 86 = 120; 34, 55, 23: 100; = 220; 10s: 10, 10, = 25

Then add the 10s and 100s

47, 86, 34, 55, + 23: 120, 100 = 220; 10, 10 = 25; total 245

Remember, when you are looking for easy pairs in the list, think about using these strategies:

Doubles	Near doubles
Rainbow facts	Bridge through 10 or 100

Spotting **rainbow pairs** to 10 and 100 is really useful when adding lists of numbers.

We practise

Add these lists of numbers using sideways chunking.

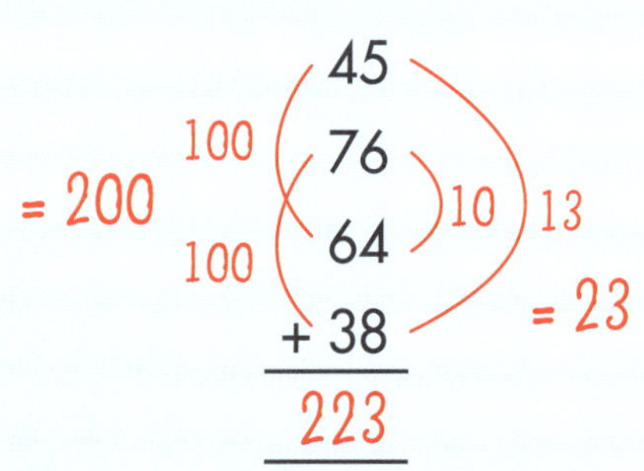

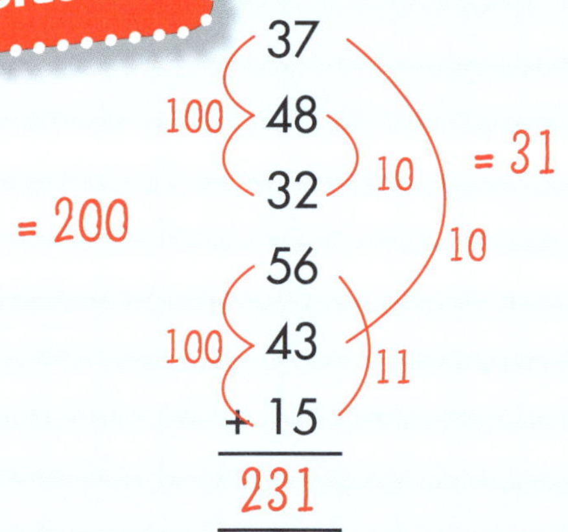

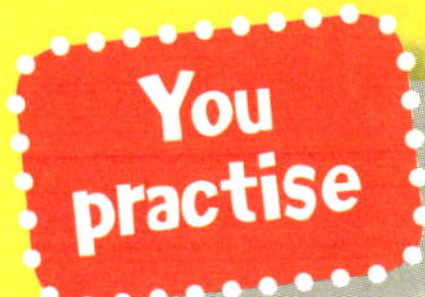

Show how to add these lists of numbers using sideways chunking.

36
25
53
+ 44

27
54
32
+ 44

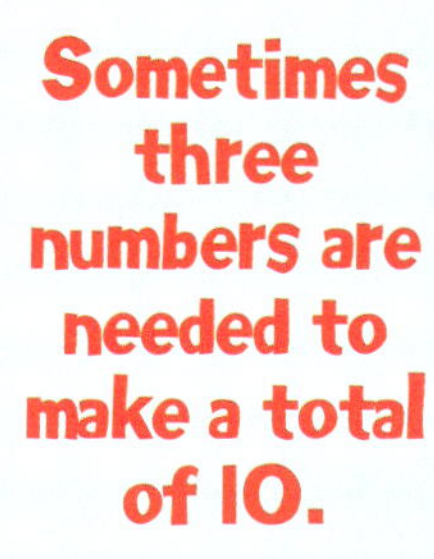

93
95
27
+ 35

54
47
12
+ 31

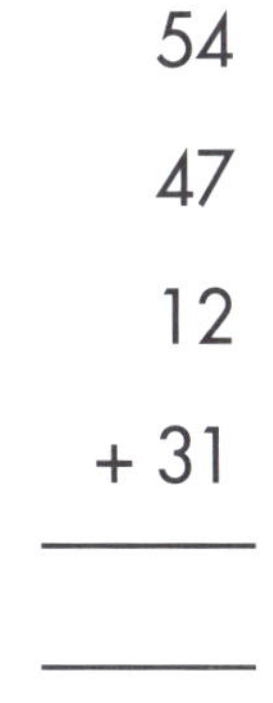

19
34
51
+ 26

35
35
64
+ 47

27
46
34
53
+ 68

39
76
45
43
+ 27

UNIT 15

MISSING DIGITS

Homework tastes like pizza!

Have you ever tried using this as an excuse for not handing in your homework?

Sorry, the dog ate my homework!

Well, suppose it was true and this is what was left after the dog had chewed your homework.

How can you find the missing digits?

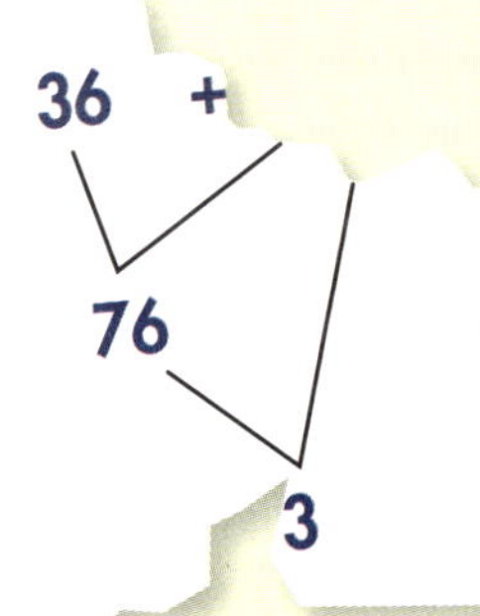

You can see that something was added to 36 to make 76.

Question: 36 + what = 76?

Answer: 36 + 40 = 76

You can see that there is a 3 in the 1s position in the answer.

Question: 6 + what = a number that ends in 3?

Answer: 6 + 7 = 13

So you now know what the missing digits are and what the homework looked like before it became a dog's dinner.

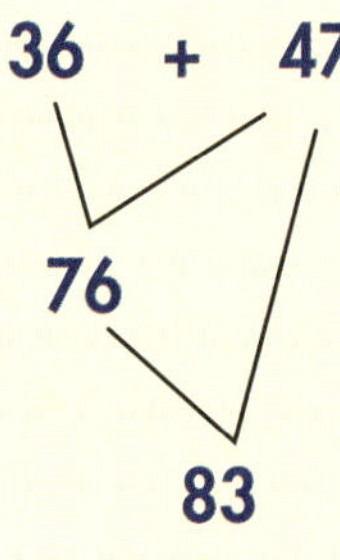

We practise

What are the missing digits in this addition?

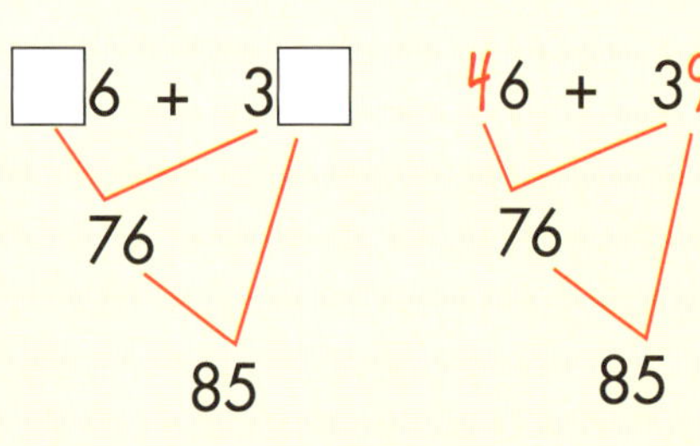

What are the missing digits in this subtraction?

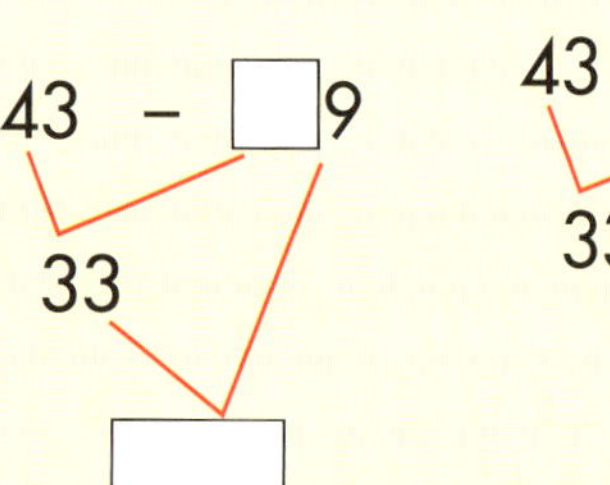

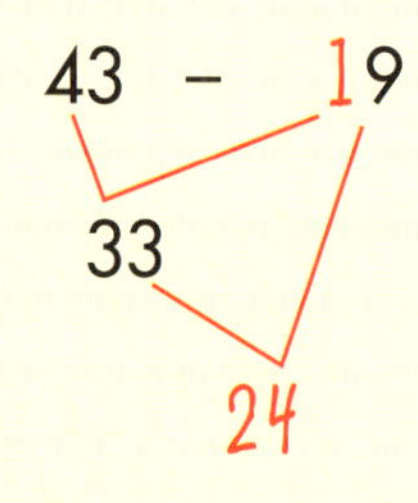

What are the missing digits in each addition?

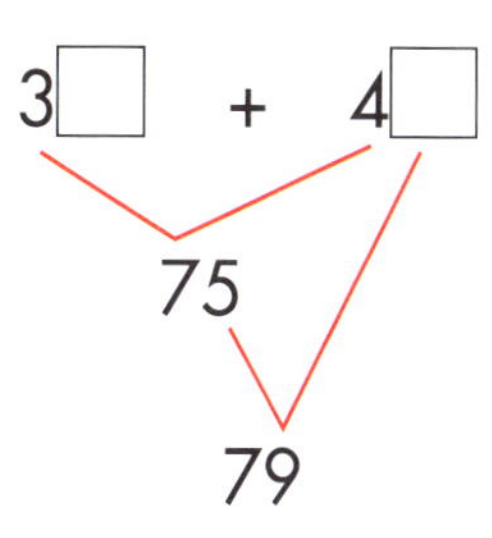

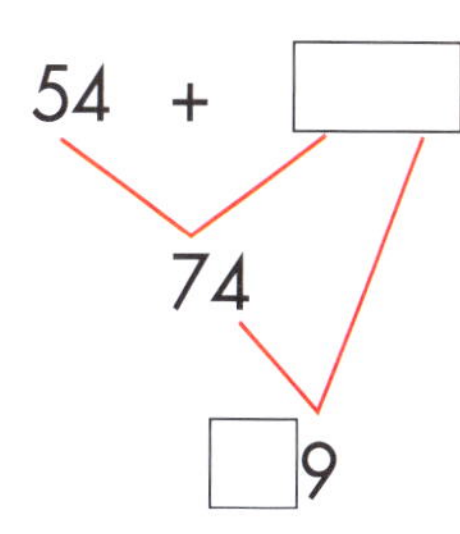

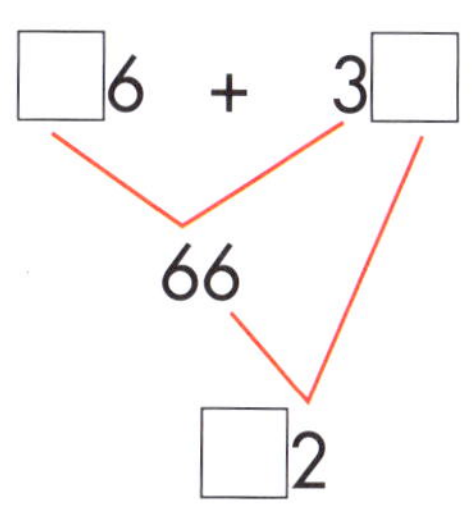

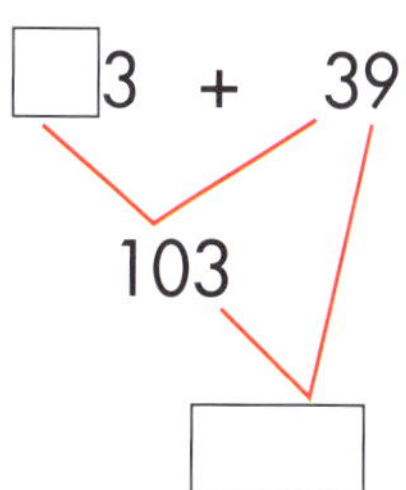

What are the missing digits in each subtraction?

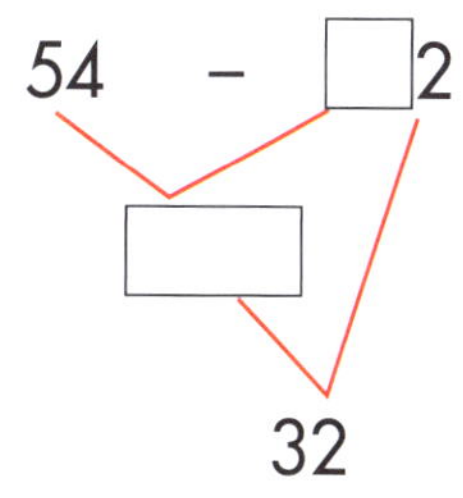

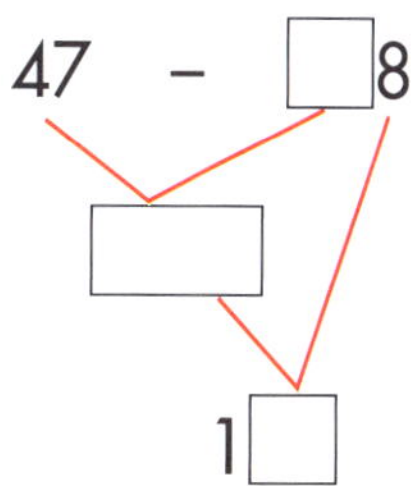

Remember to bridge back through 10 for these.

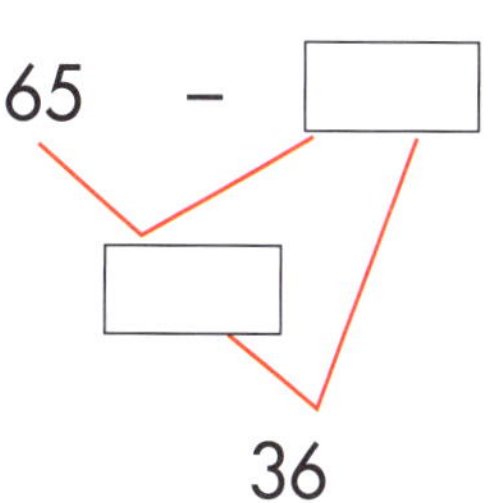

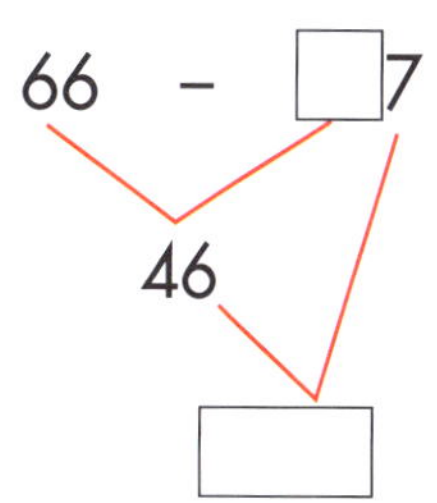

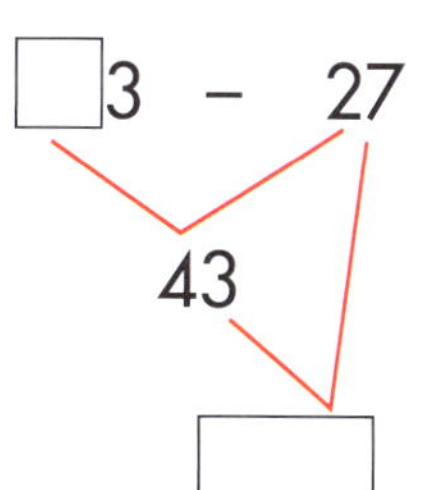

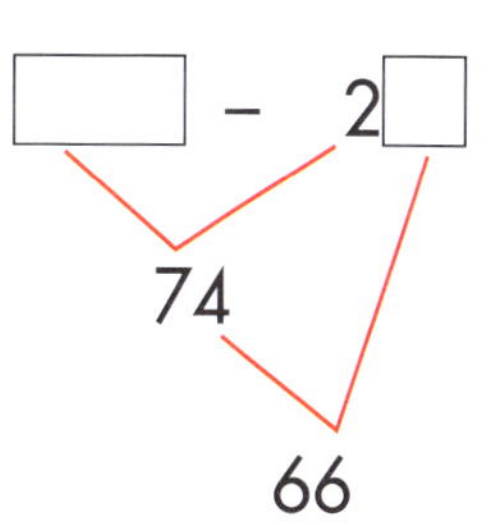

BOB time!

ADDING DECIMALS

When learning how to add decimals it is important to understand how to work with tenths.

For example, you know:

6·5 is the same as six and five tenths

7·8 is the same as seven and eight tenths

So to work out **6·5 + 7·8**, you can add the decimal parts (0·5 and 0·8) by using a **fill-up strategy on tenth grids**.

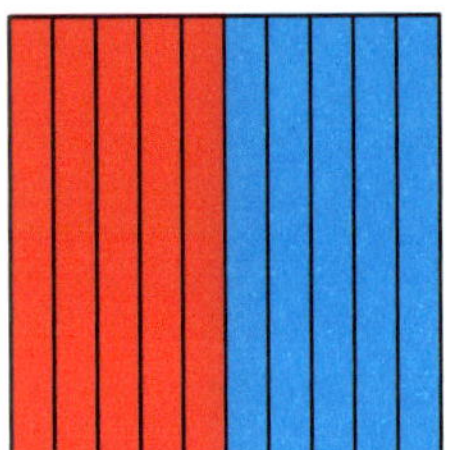
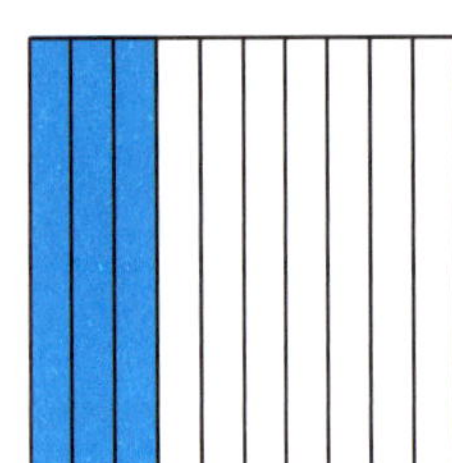

0·5 + 0·8 equals **one full grid** and **three tenths** of a grid. In decimals, this is **0·5 + 0·8 = 1·3.**

So this is how to finish working out 6·5 + 7·8.

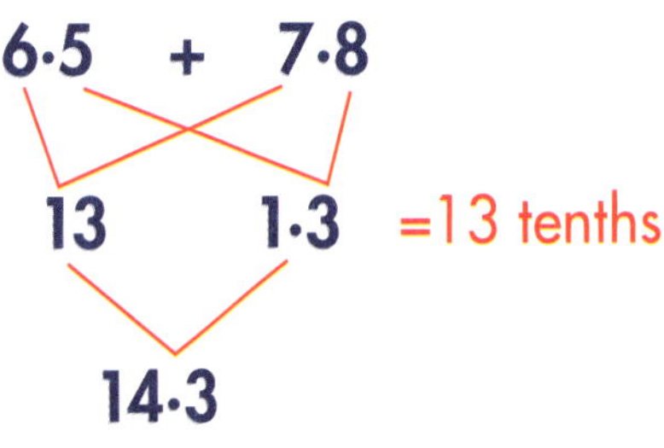

When you add the tenths, remember that
10 tenths = 1
20 tenths = 2

We practise

Show how to work out these additions by using tenths.

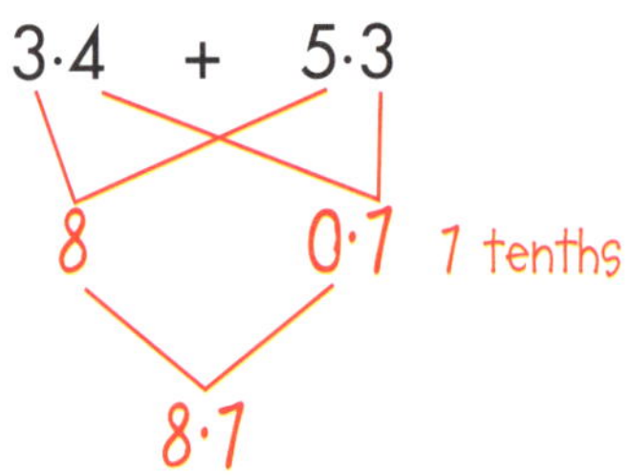

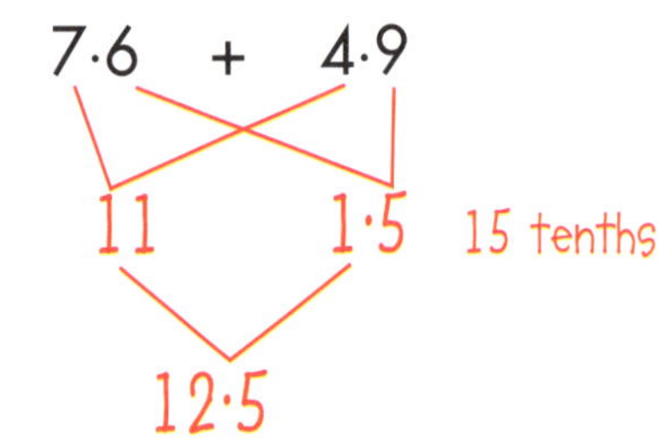

You practise

Show how to work out each addition by using tenths.

1. 3·4 + 7·3

_____ _____

_____

2. 3·5 + 8·4

_____ _____

_____

3. 4·7 + 4·2

_____ _____

_____

4. 6·4 + 5·4

_____ _____

_____

5. 3·7 + 4·6

_____ _____

_____

6. 4·5 + 6·7

_____ _____

_____

Remember to add the tenths and then change the total to a decimal number.

7. 5·7 + 6·4

_____ _____

_____

8. 6·6 + 7·8

_____ _____

_____

9. 4·8 + 3·2

_____ _____

_____

10. 26·6 + 3·9

_____ _____

_____

BOB time!

SUBTRACTING DECIMALS

Thinking in tenths also helps when learning to subtract decimals.

Using the count back strategy on an empty number line is a good way to work out a subtraction such as **3·5 – 2·6**.

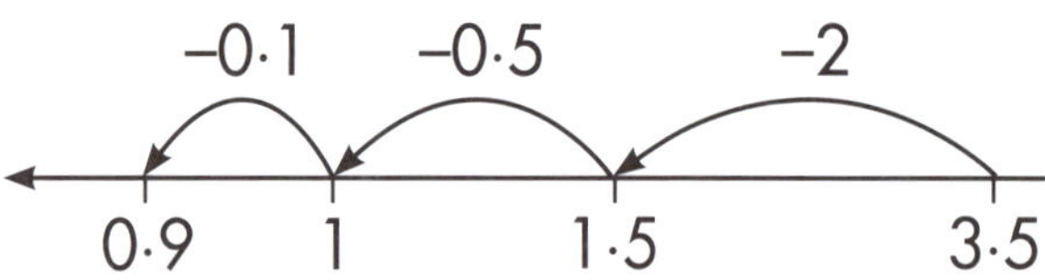

To subtract 0·1 from 1, think of the 1 as 10 tenths and 0·1 as 1 tenth. Then it is easy to see that:

$$\frac{10}{10} - \frac{1}{10} = \frac{9}{10}$$

You can also find the difference between 2·6 and 3·5 by **adding** (counting on) on an empty number line. Here's how:

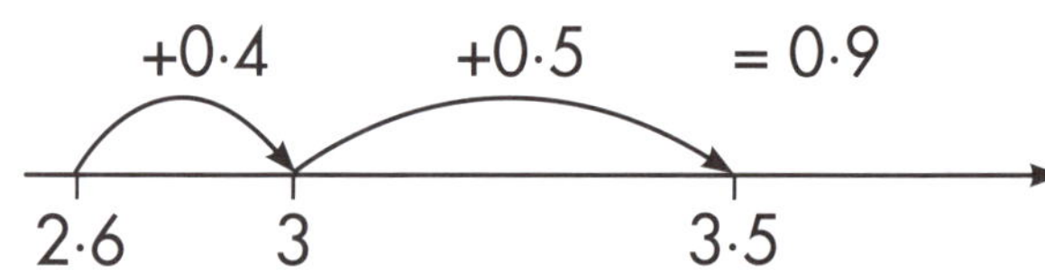

We practise

Work out 4·6 – 2·7 using the count back strategy on an empty number line.

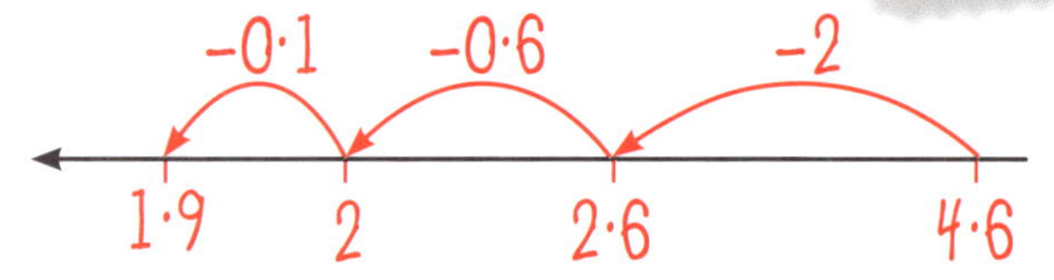

Find the difference between 2·7 and 4·6 using the count on strategy on an empty number line.

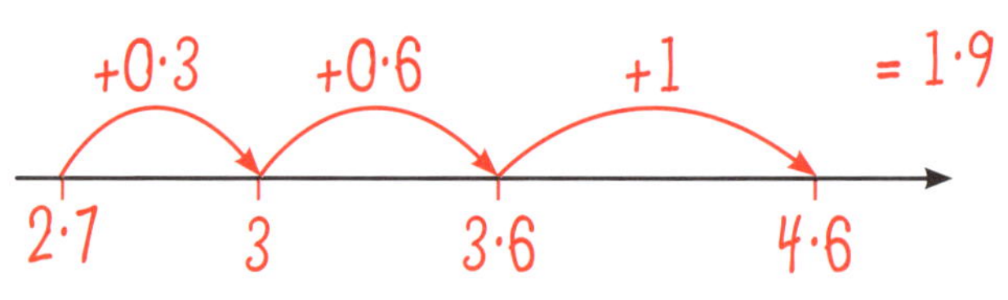

You practise

Work out each subtraction using the count back strategy on an empty number line.

1. 4·7 – 2·6

2. 5·3 – 3·6

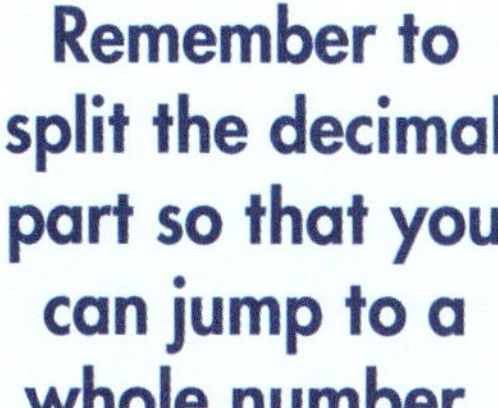

3. 6·4 – 2·8

4. 3·8 – 1·9

5. 7·4 – 6·8

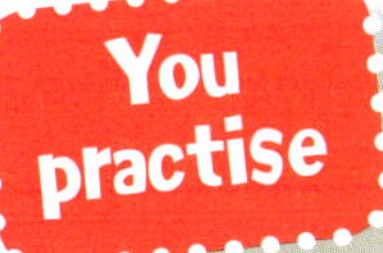

Work out the difference between each pair of numbers using the count on strategy on an empty number line.

6. 2·6 and 4·7

7. 3·6 and 5·3

8. 2·8 and 6·4

9. 1·9 and 3·8

BOB time!

10. 6·8 and 7·4

ADDITION and SUBTRACTION PATTERNS

Can you spot the **addition pattern** in this sequence of numbers?

1 11 21 31 41 …

Did you notice that it **adds 10** each time?

This **subtraction pattern** is also easy to spot.

72 62 52 42 32 …

Did you notice that it has a **count back** 10 pattern?

Now look at this – this addition pattern is not quite so easy to spot.

7 9 12 16 21 …

Here is a strategy that can help you to spot this pattern.

+2 +3 +4 +5 +?

7 9 12 16 21 ?

The next step in this pattern will be +6, so the next number will be 27.

If you **mark the jumps** and **label** them, you will soon see what the pattern is.

Labelling the jumps works for count back patterns as well.

We practise

Continue this count on pattern. Draw and label the jumps.

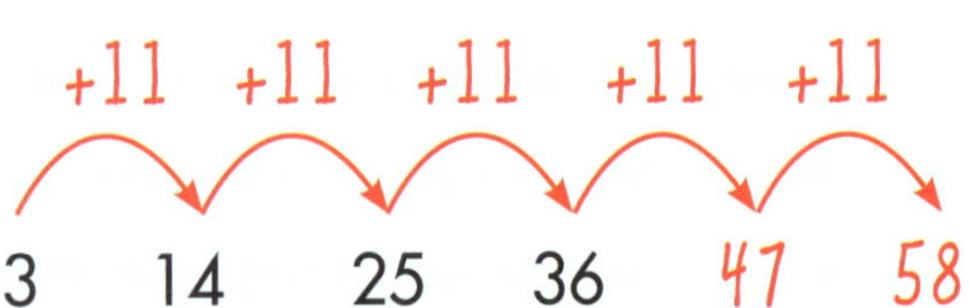

Continue this count back pattern. Draw and label the jumps.

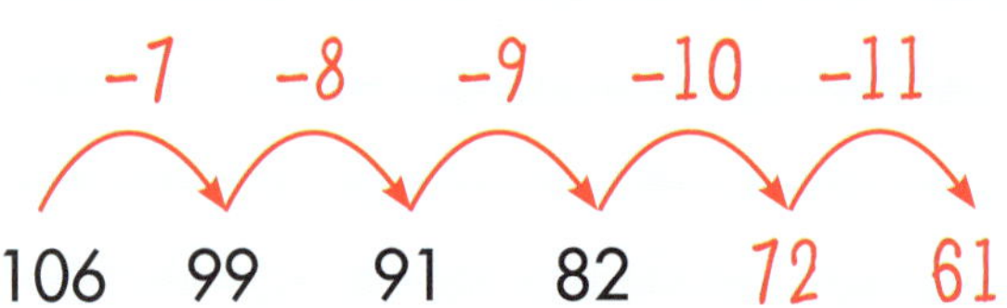

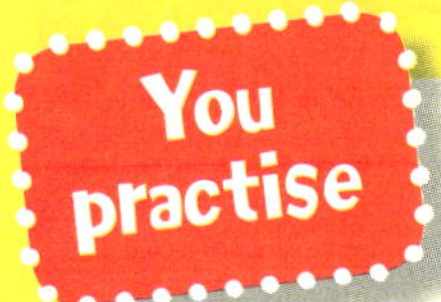

Continue these count on patterns. Draw and label the jumps.

Remember to mark the jumps. It will help you find what the pattern is.

3 6 12 24 ____ ____

2 5 9 14 ____ ____

13 22 31 40 ____ ____

0 9 19 30 ____ ____

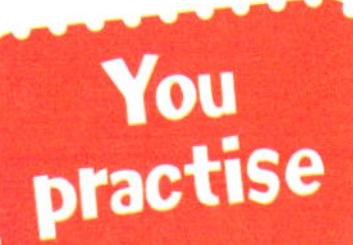

Continue these count back patterns. Draw and label the jumps.

101 91 81 71 ____ ____

101 90 79 68 ____ ____

75 72 68 63 ____ ____

222 202 183 165 ____ ____

DECIMAL ADDITION and SUBTRACTION PATTERNS

This **decimal addition pattern** is easy to spot.

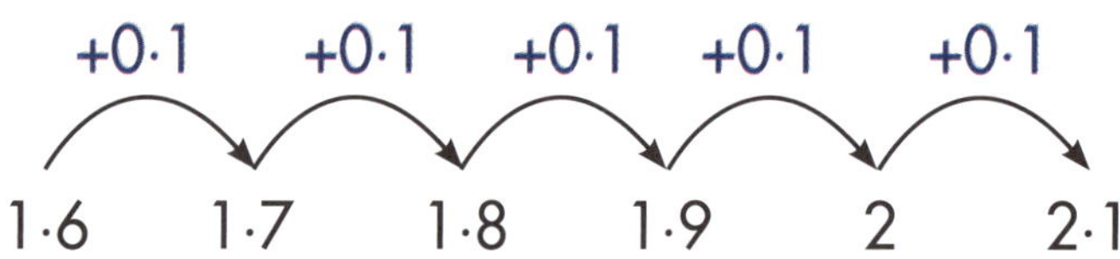

It is easy because it **counts on** 0·1 each time.

Look at this count back pattern.

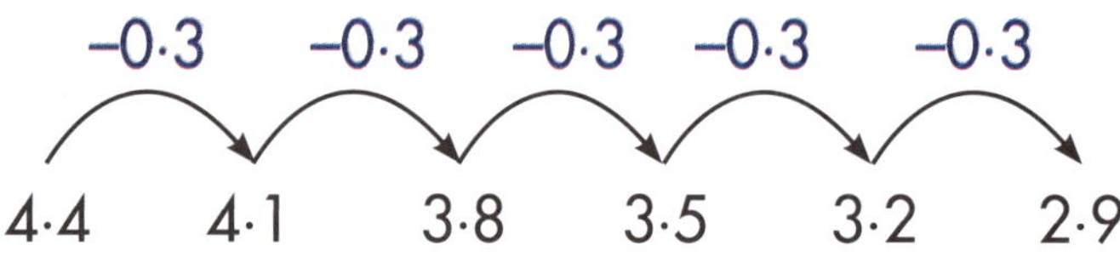

Marking and labelling the jumps makes it much easier to find the pattern.

The tricky part with decimal patterns is bridging through a whole number. For example, if you want to work out **4·1 – 0·3**, you could use a **bridge back through 4**. First split the 0·3 into 0·1 + 0·2 and show the bridge back like this.

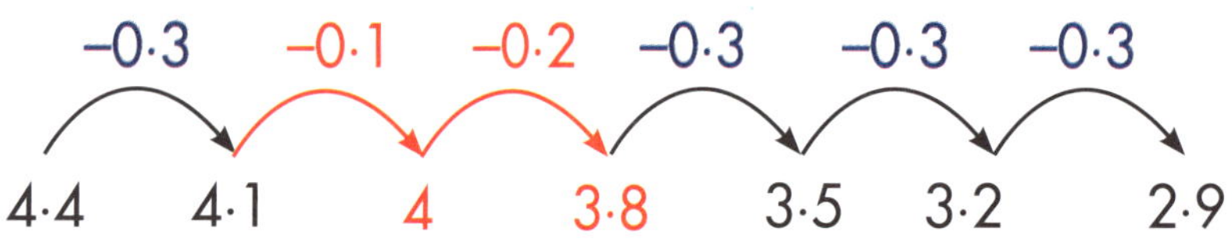

We practise

Continue this decimal count on pattern. Draw and label the jumps.

+0·2 +0·2 +0·2 +0·2 +0·2

1·3 1·5 1·7 1·9 2·1 2·3

Continue this decimal count back pattern. Draw and label the jumps.

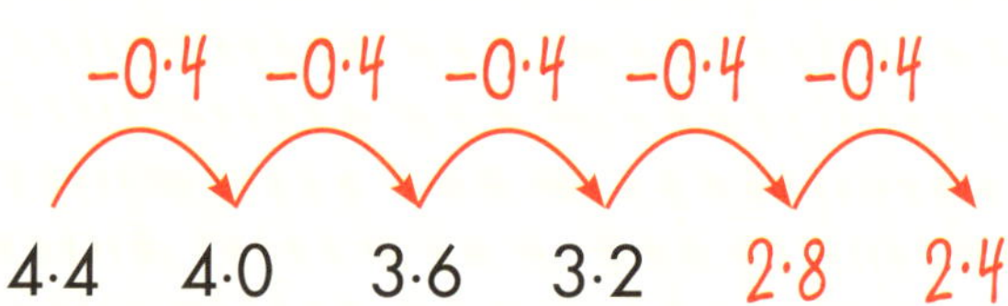

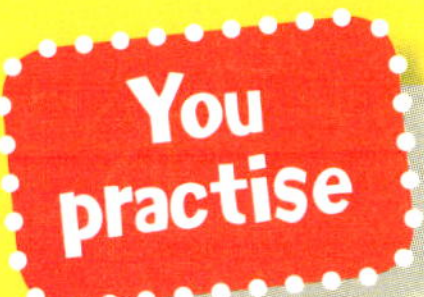

Complete these decimal count on patterns. Draw and label the jumps.

Remember to mark the jumps and label them to find the pattern.

1·5 1·8 2·1 2·4 ____ ____

3·2 3·7 4·2 4·7 ____ ____

1·6 2·2 2·8 3·4 ____ ____

1·2 2·3 3·4 4·5 ____ ____

Complete these decimal count back patterns. Draw and label the jumps.

5·3 5 4·7 4·4 ____ ____

6·6 6·2 5·8 5·4 ____ ____

9 8·6 8·1 7·5 ____ ____

3·7 3·2 2·8 2·5 ____ ____

MORE PROBLEM SOLVING

Jake and Clare are playing Closest to 7·5.

To do this, they each draw two cards from a pack that has only the numbers 1 – 9 with the ace counting as 1. Clare draws 6 and 5 to make 6·5. Jake draws 8 and 3 to make 8·3. Who is closer to 7·5 and by how much?

Notice that the important information is highlighted in blue and what has to be found out is highlighted in pink.

One way to solve this problem is using an empty number line.

Clare

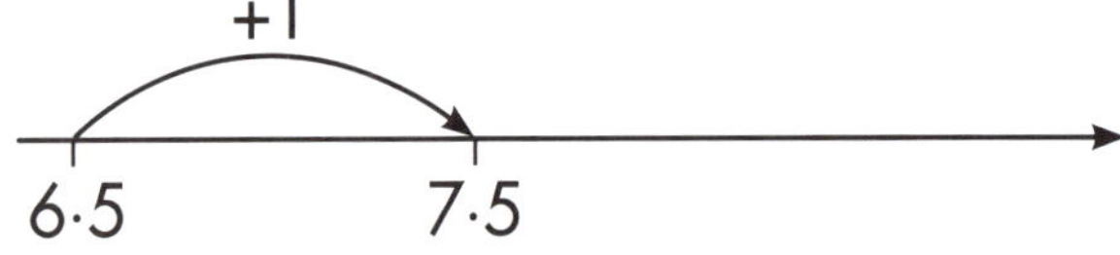

Jake

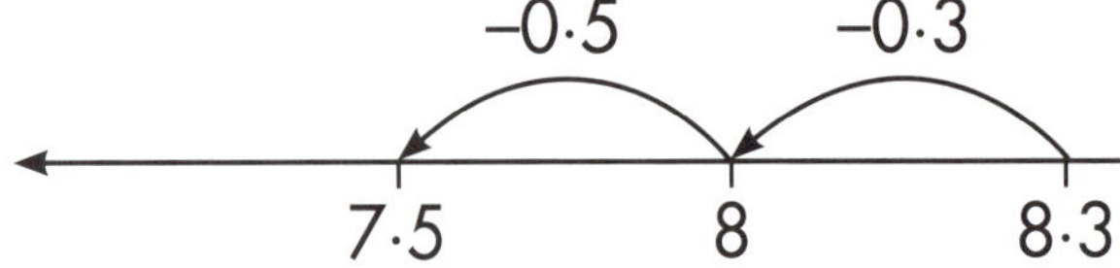

Clare is 1 away from 7·5 and Jake is 0·8 away.
So Jake is closer by 0·2.

Think of Jake's jumps as $\frac{3}{10}$ and $\frac{5}{10}$, making $\frac{8}{10}$ altogether.

We practise

Highlight the important information and what you have to find in this problem. Use an empty number line to work out your answer.

While playing *Closest to 7·5*, Clare draws 9 and 4 and Jake draws 5 and 4. What decimal number do they each have? Who is closer to 7·5?

Jake

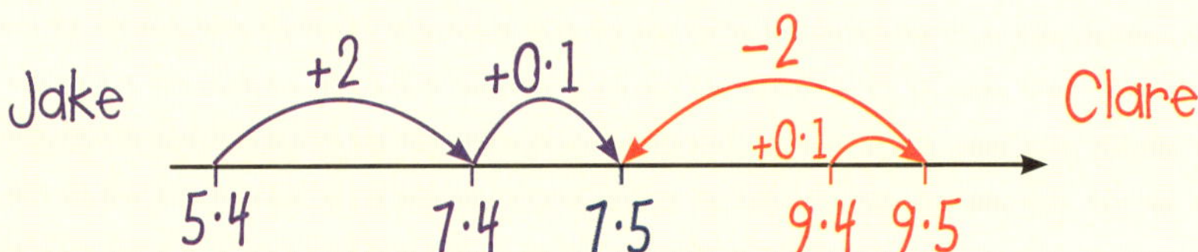

Clare

Answer: Clare has 9·4 and Jake has 5·4. Clare is closer to 7·5 by 0·2.

Highlight the important information and what you have to find in these problems, then answer them.

1. Jake scores 356 and 275 in pinball. Clare scores 288 and 329. Who is in the lead and by how much?

___

2. In a game of darts, players start with 301 and subtract their scores until they reach 0. Jake has scored 35 and 25 so far and Clare has scored 47 and 24. How much do they both still need to score to reach 0?

___

3. Mrs Smith is 76. Mrs Harrison is 58. What is the difference in their ages?

___

4. In Grand Slam, players pick four numbers from a barrel. The player with the highest total wins.
Matty has picked 36, 43, 64 and 72.
Tsai has picked 43, 27, 46 and 54.
What are their totals and who won the Grand Slam?

___

___

5. What are the missing digits?

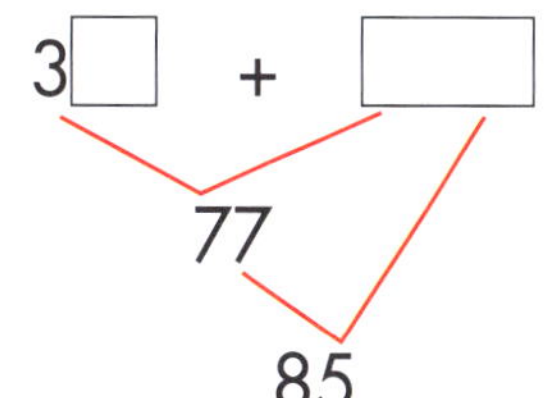

6. Matty and Jake are playing fill-up the five decimal grids. Matty has scored 1·6 and 2·5 and Jake has scored 2·3 and 1·4. Who has filled the most of the grids and by how much?

___

7. How much do Matty and Jake each need to score to fill their grids?

___

___

8. 1000 raffle tickets have been sold. 365 were sold by the school, 278 were sold at the supermarket and the rest were sold at the cinema.
How many raffle tickets were sold at the cinema?

___

9. Continue Clare's number pattern. Mark and label the jumps.

11 13 17 23 ___ ___

10. Continue Jake's number pattern. Mark and label the jumps.

5·4 6·2 7 7·8 ___ ___

BOB time!

TEST 1

Write the answer and the strategy you could use for each addition.

50 + 60 = ______

(______________________________)

70 + 30 = ______

(______________________________)

80 + 50 = ______

(______________________________)

Show how to round and adjust for this addition.

28 + 33 + 45

Round _____ + _____ + _____ = _____

Adjust _____ + _____ = _____

Round these numbers to the nearest 10.

38 _____ 42 _____ 35 _____
98 _____

Show how to use landmark numbers to complete this addition.

27 + 78

Number split and chunk for this addition.

57 + 35

Round and adjust for this subtraction.

48 – 29

Round _____ – _____ = _____

Adjust _____ + _____ = _____

Show how to add 36 + 49 on an empty number line.

Show two ways of subtracting 38 from 67 on an empty number line.

TEST 2

Use the front-end method for these additions.

$$\begin{array}{r} 265 \\ +\ 336 \\ \hline \end{array} \qquad \begin{array}{r} 343 \\ +\ 427 \\ \hline \end{array}$$

______ ______

______ ______

Use number splitting for this subtraction.

$$\begin{array}{r} 357 \\ -\ 148 \\ \hline \end{array}$$

______

______

What is the difference between 58 and 75? Use a count on strategy on an empty number line.

Add this list of numbers using sideways chunking.

$$\begin{array}{r} 96 \\ 24 \\ 47 \\ +\ 13 \\ \hline \end{array}$$

______

What are the missing numbers in this subtraction?

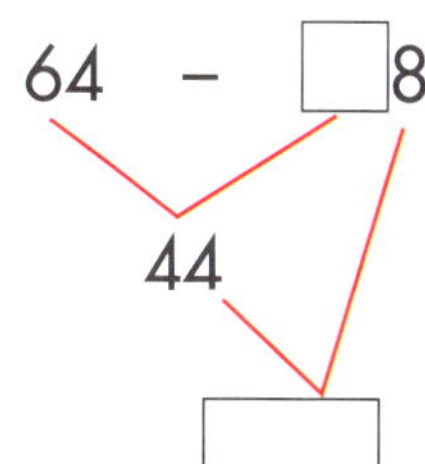

Work out this addition using tenths.

3·7 + 5·9

______ ______

______

Show the subtraction 5·6 – 3·8 on the empty number line.

What is the difference between 2·8 and 5·7? Use a count on strategy on an empty number line.

Continue this count-on pattern.

7 10 14 19 ______ ______

Continue this count-back pattern.

3·9 3·5 3·1 2·7 ______ ______

ANSWERS

Unit 1

1 20 + 20 + 10 = 50, 30 + 30 – 10 = 50
2 40 + 40 + 10 = 90, 50 + 50 – 10 = 90
3 60 + 60 + 10 = 130, 70 + 70 – 10 = 130
4 80 + 80 + 10 = 170, 90 + 90 – 10 = 170
5 60 + 40 = 100(rf)
6 70 + 70 = 140(d)
7 60 + 50 = 110(nd)
8 80 + 20 = 100(rf)
9 30 + 30 = 60(d)
10 70 + 80 = 150(nd)

Unit 2

1 8 + 2 + 3 = 13
2 9 + 1 + 4 = 14
3 7 + 3 + 2 = 12
4 8 + 2 + 4 = 14
5 90 + 10 + 40 = 140
6 80 + 20 + 10 = 110
7 70 + 30 + 16 = 116
8 80 + 20 + 57 = 157

Unit 3

1 40 + 40 = 80, An estimate is 80
2 30 + 50 = 80, An estimate is 80
3 70 + 50 = 120, An estimate is 120
4 70 + 60 = 130, An estimate is 130
5 30 + 40 + 40 = 110, An estimate is 110
6 40 + 30 + 30 = 100, An estimate is 100
7 40 + 60 + 60 = 160, An estimate is 160
8 30 + 20 + 20 = 70, An estimate is 70
9 60 + 70 + 30 = 160, An estimate is 160
10 100 + 50 + 50 = 200, An estimate is 200

Unit 4

1 + 1
40 + 27 = 67
67 – 1 = 66

2 + 2
20 + 26 = 46
46 – 2 = 44

3 + 3
30 + 35 = 65
65 – 3 = 62

4 + 2
30 + 54 = 84
84 – 2 = 82

5 – 2
20 + 36 = 56
56 + 2 = 58

6 – 1
30 + 47 = 77
77 + 1 = 78

7 71
8 63
9 71
10 79

Unit 5

1 1 + 25 + 75 + 2 = 103
100
2 1 + 50 + 25 + 2 = 78
75
3 3 + 75 + 75 + 1 = 154
150
4 1 + 50 + 75 + 1 = 127
125
5 3 + 250 + 250 + 1 = 504
500
6 3 + 500 + 500 + 6 = 1009
1000
7 1 + 750 + 250 + 3 = 1004
1000
8 2 + 750 + 500 + 3 = 1255
1250

Unit 6

1 56 + 30 = 86, 86 + 3 = 89
2 38 + 20 = 58, 58 + 4 = 62
3 27 + 60 = 87, 87 + 8 = 95
4 64 + 20 = 84, 84 + 9 = 93
5 37 + 40 = 77, 77 + 6 = 83
6 52 + 60 = 112, 112 + 8 = 120
7 40 + 70 = 110
9
119
8 30 + 20 = 50
15
65
9 150 + 50 = 200
14
214
10 230 + 60 = 290
14
304

Unit 7

1 Round 55 – 30 = 25, Adjust 25 + 1 = 26
2 Round 76 – 30 = 46, Adjust 46 + 2 = 48
3 Round 57 – 40 = 17, Adjust 17 + 2 = 19
4 Round 63 – 30 = 33, Adjust 33 + 3 = 36
5 Round 82 – 60 = 22, Adjust 22 + 2 = 24
6 Round 77 – 30 = 47, Adjust 47 + 1 = 48
7 Round 37 – 20 = 17, Adjust 17 + 1 = 18
8 Round 46 – 30 = 16, Adjust 16 + 3 = 19
9 Round 93 – 50 = 43, Adjust 43 – 4 = 39
10 Round 87 – 50 = 37, Adjust 37 – 5 = 32

ANSWERS

Unit 8

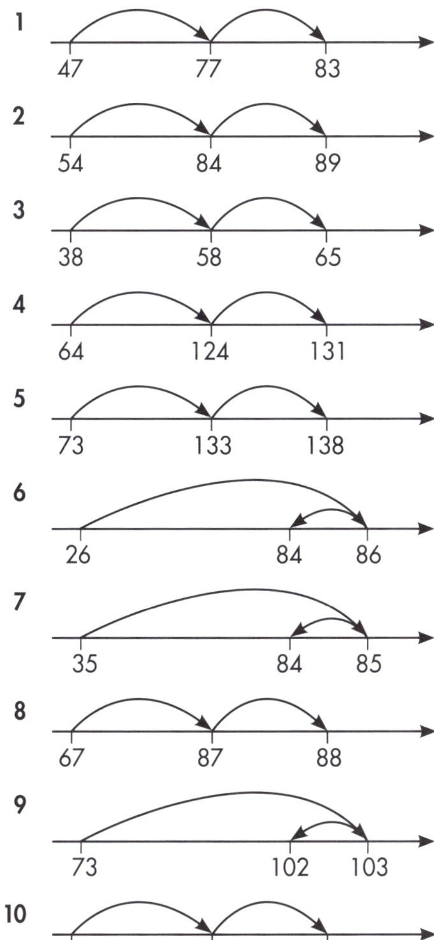

Unit 9

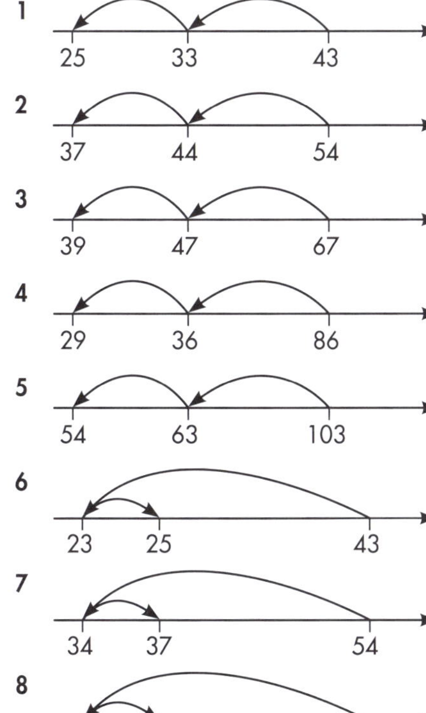

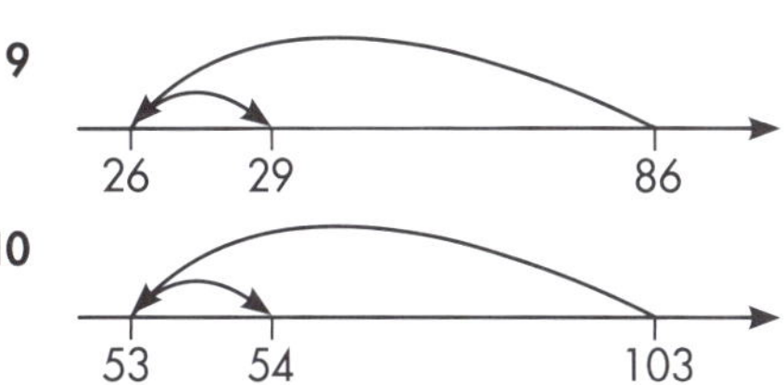

Unit 10

1. 95 collector cards altogether
2. Matty is in the lead by 2
3. Clare does not have enough money
4. Jake and Matty have to pay $45
5. Jake was closest by 20
6. Clare and Jake will lose by 13
7. Clare had $47
8. Matty's third card is worth 52
9. Rebecca has 84 left
10. 33 days until the party

Unit 11

1
$$\begin{array}{r} 400 \\ +\ \ 60 \\ 8 \\ \hline 468 \end{array}$$

4
$$\begin{array}{r} 500 \\ +110 \\ 8 \\ \hline 618 \end{array}$$

2
$$\begin{array}{r} 500 \\ +100 \\ 9 \\ \hline 609 \end{array}$$

5
$$\begin{array}{r} 400 \\ +100 \\ 16 \\ \hline 516 \end{array}$$

3
$$\begin{array}{r} 500 \\ +\ \ 70 \\ 11 \\ \hline 581 \end{array}$$

6
$$\begin{array}{r} 400 \\ +100 \\ 15 \\ \hline 515 \end{array}$$

7
$$\begin{array}{r} 460 \\ +\ \ \ 8 \\ \hline 468 \end{array}$$

9
$$\begin{array}{r} 500 \\ +\ \ 15 \\ \hline 515 \end{array}$$

8
$$\begin{array}{r} 300 \\ +\ \ 14 \\ \hline 314 \end{array}$$

10
$$\begin{array}{r} 1010 \\ +\ \ \ 12 \\ \hline 1022 \end{array}$$

ANSWERS

Unit 12

1 465 – 300 leaves 165
165 – 20 leaves 145
145 – 3 leaves 142

2 534 – 100 leaves 434
434 – 20 leaves 414
434 – 6 (2 + 4) leaves 408

3 367 – 100 leaves 267
267 – 40 leaves 227
227 – 8 (7 + 1) leaves 219

4 656 – 200 leaves 456
456 – 30 leaves 426
426 – 8 (6 + 2) leaves 418

5 735 – 400 leaves 335
335 – 10 leaves 325
325 – 9 (5 + 4) leaves 316

6 673 – 400 leaves 273
273 – 20 leaves 253
253 – 7 (3 + 4) leaves 246

7		8	
	324		238
	294		188
	288		179

Unit 13

1 27 30 40 42 — The difference is 15

2 45 50 60 68 — The difference is 23

3 37 40 110 116 — The difference is 79

4 27 30 40 42 — The difference is 15

5 45 65 68 — The difference is 23

6 37 40 110 116 — The difference is 79

Unit 14

1	158	5	157
2	250	6	144
3	130	7	181
4	228	8	230

Unit 15

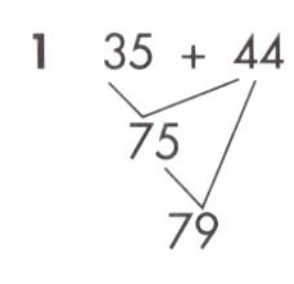

1 35 + 44
75
79

3 54 + 25
74
79

2 36 + 36
66
72

4 73 + 39
103
112

5 54 – 22
34
32

8 47 – 28
27
19

6 65 – 29
45
36

9 66 – 27
46
39

7 63 – 27
43
36

10 94 – 28
74
66

Unit 16

1 10 + 0·7 (7 tenths)
10·7

2 11 + 0·9 (9 tenths)
11·9

3 8 + 0·9 (9 tenths)
8·9

4 11 + 0·8 (8 tenths)
11·8

5 7 + 1·3 (13 tenths)
8·3

6 10 + 1·2 (12 tenths)
11·2

7 11 + 1·1 (11 tenths)
12·3

8 13 + 1·4 (14 tenths)
14·4

9 7 + 1·0 (10 tenths)
8

10 29 + 1·5 (15 tenths)
30·5

Unit 17

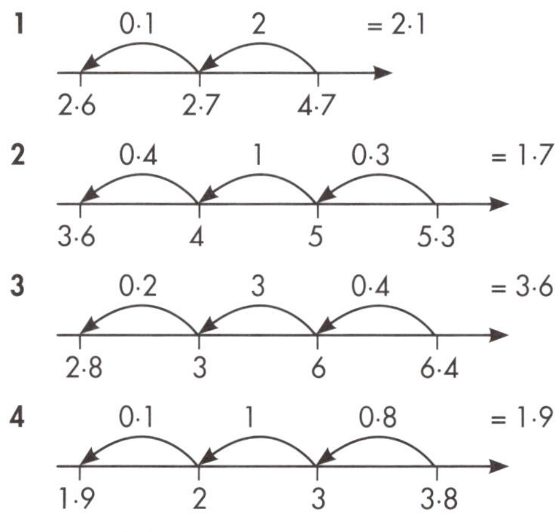

ANSWERS

6 0·4 1 0·7 = 2·1
2·6 3 4 4·7

7 0·4 1 0·3 = 1·7
3·6 4 5 5·3

8 0·2 3 0·4 = 3·6
2·8 3 6 6·4

9 0·1 1 0·8 = 1·9
1·9 2 3 3·8

10 0·2 0·4 = 0·6
6·8 7 7·4

Unit 18

1	3	6	12	24	48	96
2	2	5	9	14	20	27
3	13	22	31	40	49	58
4	0	9	19	30	42	55
5	101	91	81	71	61	51
6	101	90	79	68	57	46
7	75	72	68	63	57	50
8	222	202	183	165	148	132

Unit 19

1 2·7 3 **2** 5·2 5·7
3 4 4·6 **4** 5·6 6·7
5 4·1 3·8 **6** 5 4·6
7 6·8 6 **8** 2·3 2·2

Unit 20

1. Jake by 14
2. Jakes needs 241, Clare needs 230
3. 18 years
4. Matty has 215 and Tsai has 170
   Matty won the Grand Slam
5. 37 + 48
6. Matty by 0.4
7. Matty needs 0.9, Jake needs 1.3
8. 357
9. Clare: +2 +4 +6 +8 +10

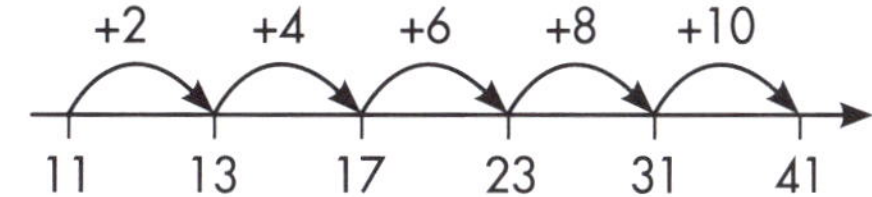

10 Jake: +0·8 +0·8 +0·8 +0·8 +0·8
5·4 6·2 7 7·8 8·6 9·4

Test 1

1. 110 (near double), 100 (rainbow fact), 130 (bridge through 100)
2. Round: 30 + 30 + 45 = 105, Adjust: 105 + 1 = 106
3. 40, 40, 40, 100
4. 25 + 2 + 75 + 3 = 105
5. 57 + 35
   57 + 30 = 87
   87 + 5 = 92
6. Round: 48 – 30 = 18, Adjust: 18 + 1 = 19
7. 36 + 4 = 40 + 40 = 80 + 5 = 85
8. –1 –30 –7
   29 30 60 67

   2 20 7 = 29

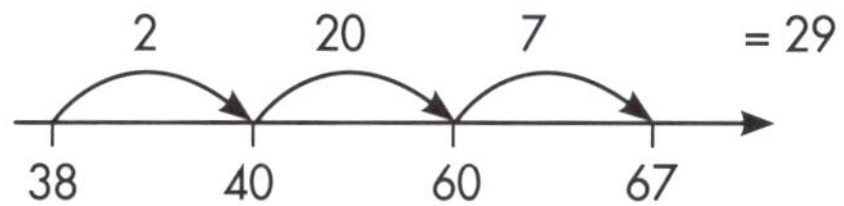

Test 2

1

```
  5 0 0        7 0 0
+   9 0      +   6 0
    1 1          1 0
  6 0 1        7 7 0
```

2 357 – 100 leaves 257
257 – 40 leaves 217
217 – 8 leaves 209

3 58 60 70 75
The difference is 17

4 180

5 64 – 28 = 36

6 8 + 1·6 = 9·6

7 0·2 1 0·6 = 1·8
3·8 4 5 5·6

8 0·2 2 0·7 = 2·9
2·8 3 5 5·7

9 25 32

10 2·3 1·9

Back to Basics Addition and Subtraction Years 4 and 5

Copyright © 2013 Blake Education
Reprinted 2018

ISBN: 978 1 74215 931 7

Published by Pascal Press
PO Box 250
Glebe NSW 2037
www.pascalpress.com.au
contact@pascalpress.com.au

Author: Ann Baker
Publisher: Lynn Dickinson
Editors: Eliza Hope, Ruth Schultz
Design and illustration: Janice Bowles
Cover design: Deb Snibson, MAPG
Printed by Thumbprints

Reproduction and communication for educational purposes
The Australian Copyright Act 1968 (the Act) allows a maximum of one chapter or 10% of the pages of this work, whichever is the greater, to be reproduced and/or communicated by any educational institution for its educational purposes provided that the educational institution (or that body that administers it) has given a remuneration notice to the Copyright Agency Limited (CAL) under the Act.
For details of the CAL licence for educational institutions contact:
Copyright Agency Limited
Level 15, 233 Castlereagh Street
Sydney, NSW 2000

Reproduction and communication for other purposes
Except as permitted under the Act (for example a fair dealing for the purpose of study, research, criticism or review) no part of this book may be reproduced, stored in a retrieval system, communicated or transmitted in any form or by any means without prior written permission. All inquiries should be made to the publisher at the address above.
© Australian Curriculum, Assessment and Reporting Authority 2010.
This is a modified extract from the Australian Curriculum. ACARA neither endorses nor verifies the accuracy of the information provided and accepts no responsibility for incomplete or inaccurate information. You can find the unaltered and most up to date version of this material at http://www.australiancurriculum.edu.au/Home
This modified material is reproduced with the permission of ACARA.